THINKERS OF OUR TIME

G K CHESTERTON

THINKERS OF
OUR TIME

G K CHESTERTON

Ian Crowther

The Claridge Press
London

First published in Great Britain 1991

by The Claridge Press
6 Linden Gardens
London W2 4ES
and Box 420
Lexington
Georgia 30648

Copyright © Ian Crowther

Typeset by

and printed by
Short Run Press
Exeter, Devon

ISBN 1-870626-81-8   (Hardback)
ISBN 1-870626-86-9   (Paperback)

Crowther, Ian: *G K Chesterton*

1. Political Science

CONTENTS

PREFACE

Even the most devoted reader of Chesterton might wonder what can possibly justify another book about him. Writings about Chesterton may not yet have exceeded in number those by Chesterton; even so, within the short space of the last eight years there have appeared three substantial biographies. But despite such attention, few of Chesterton's books remain in print. Moreover, outside the relatively small circle of his admirers, Chesterton today exists in most people's minds, if he exists at all, in fragments. He is remembered as the creator of the Father Brown stories; or as the poet who wrote 'Lepanto', 'The Ballad of the White Horse', and one or two other pieces; or as the champion of an outdated politico-economic theory called Distributism; or as the Catholic apologist; or as one half of the pantomime creature, the ChesterBelloc; or, simply, as the absent-minded eccentric who sent a telegram to his wife which read: "am in Market Harborough. Where ought I to be?" To see Chesterton whole is no easy task, especially as he was, of course, all these things. But not only were all these things the characteristics of one man. All of them in some way reflected a particular vision of the world, which it has been the misfortune of most moderns not to share. It is this vision which animated just about everything that Chesterton wrote and did. It is this vision which I here attempt to explain. And if justification there be for this book, it is perhaps this: that in works about Chesterton we generally learn a great deal more about the life of the man than the life of the mind. This work has been conceived with the object of redressing that balance a little, by rendering Chesterton's thoughts intelligible to the modern reader. I do not underestimate the difficulty of the task, since there is no

natural affinity between the modern mind and Chesterton's. To
enter the latter is, in many respects, to enter unfamiliar territory.

This book is dedicated to my wife, Kristina, and my daughters,
Louisa and Emma, who made it possible.

Buckland Newton, February 1990.

ABBREVIATIONS

The works quoted in the text are given the following abbreviations, with the relevant page number. The date of first publication, if not of the edition cited here, is shown in parentheses.

A *Autobiography*, Hutchinson, 1950 (1937).
B *The Poetic Quality in Liberalism*, The Chesterton Review, May 1982 (1905).
C *The Mystagogue, Essays and Poems*, ed. Wilfrid Sheed, Penguin, 1958.
D *The Napoleon of Notting Hill*, John Lane, 1904.
E *The Man Who Was Thursday*, Penguin, 1967 (1908).
F *The Incredulity of Father Brown*, Harmondsworth, 1976 (1926).
G *Gilbert Keith Chesterton*, Maisie Ward, Sheed & Ward, 1944.
H *Heretics*, John Lane, 1928 (1905).
I *Orthodoxy*, The Bodley Head, 1957 (1908).
J *Eugenics and other Evils*, Wm. Collins, 1922.
K *St Francis of Assisi*, Hodder & Stoughton, 1934 (1923).
L *St Thomas Aquinas*, Hodder & Stoughton, 1943 (1933).
M *The Catholic Church and Conversion*, Burns & Oates, 1960 (1926).
N *The Thing*, Unicorn Books, 1939 (1929).
O *G F Watts*, Duckworth, 1975 (1904).
P *Chaucer*, Faber, 1962 (1932).
Q *The Everlasting Man*, Hodder & Stoughton, 1926 (1925).
R *What I saw in America*, Hodder & Stoughton, 1922.
S *The New Jerusalem*, Hodder & Stoughton, 1920.
T *A Short History of England*, Chatto & Windus, 1917.
U *Defence of the West*, Henri Massis, Faber & Gwyer, 1927.

V *What's Wrong With the World*, Cassell, 1910.
W *The Well and the Shallows*, Sheed & Ward, 1934.
X *The Superstitionof Divorce*, Chatto & Windus, 1920.
Y *The Outline of Sanity*, Methuen, 1926.

1. Chesterton the Man and Man According to Chesterton

Gilbert Keith Chesterton spent much of his life reacting against the certainties, and uncertainties, of his age. That he seemed to his contemporaries, as he still seems to us today, an eccentric, reveals as much about the character of the modern world as about Chesterton himself. Chesterton was a centric genius at a time when normality was mistaken for abnormality, and vice versa. It is true that Chesterton was sometimes not 'all there', the mind being in one place while the body was in another. The tales of his absent-mindedness are legendary, and legion. But they only go to show that here was a true contemplative, given (as few people are) to the habit of prolonged and concentrated thought. Chesterton was fortunate that the circumstances of his life allowed his imagination and intelligence free play, and this from childhood onwards.

He was born in Kensington, in 1874, of tolerant, respectable, middle-class parents, in a milieu where (as he put it) "the word 'respectability' was not yet exclusively a term of abuse, but retained some dim philological connection with the idea of being respected" (A, 10). Chesterton's father, as well as carrying on the family house agent business, pursued many unmercenary and artistic hobbies which gave pleasure as much to his family as himself. From his father Chesterton inherited a talent for drawing, in which art (together with versifying) he early excelled at St Paul's School, illustrating there his friend E C Bentley's first book of Clerihews.

During his art school years at the Slade, which he attended after St Paul's, Chesterton fell into a *fin-de-siècle* slough of despond and nihilistic despair from which he emerged only with difficulty and after working out a philosophy of life which he later came to identify with traditional Christianity. He was enormously fortified in his

new found optimism by the experience of falling in love with his
future wife, Frances Blogg; it was during their courtship that he first
began writing articles, reviews and verse. Marriage, and a home in
Battersea, came in June 1901; the publication of his first book of
essays, *The Defendant*, in October. From the Battersea flat Chesterton sallied forth into Fleet Street, where he made the great friend-
ships of his life — Belloc, Shaw, Wells, Beerbohm, among many
others. From the first Chesterton's output was prodigious. He had
a regular column in the *Liberal Daily News* and another (every week
for thirty years) in the *Illustrated London News*. These journalistic
pieces, together with a succession of books (notably *Browning*,
Dickens, and *Heretics*), swiftly established Chesterton as a man of
letters; while *Orthodoxy*, published in 1908, revealed to the world
the convictions which, fourteen years later, were to take him to
Rome.

In 1909 Frances, concerned for her husband's health, moved
them to the small Buckinghamshire town of Beaconsfield outside
London. But the flow of writing continued unabated and in 1915
Chesterton collapsed and for some months lay in a coma. Shortly
after his recovery in 1916 he took over the editorship of the *New
Witness* from his brother Cecil, who was then in the trenches. In
1918 Cecil died and Gilbert carried on the paper — and the battle his
brother had begun for political decency — for the rest of his life,
reluctantly consenting to it being renamed, in 1925, *G.K.'s Weekly*.
The paper taxed Chesterton's strength as well as his purse, and to
pay for it many of the Father Brown stories were written as
potboilers.

Chesterton was finally received into the Roman Catholic Church
in 1922, to be followed four years later by Frances. The noblest fruit
of his conversion, and the masterpiece of his mature years, was *The
Everlasting Man*, published in 1925. To this day it remains what
Chesterton intended it to be: the answer not only to H G Wells's
Outline of World History, but to all histories based on a belief in
linear progress. Many travel books and essays appeared in the
nineteen twenties and thirties as a result of Chesterton's journeys

abroad, which included visits to Holland, Palestine, Poland, Italy, Spain and the United States, in which last country he made two lecture tours. He also made a number of broadcasts for the BBC, triumphantly proving himself to be as at home in the wireless medium as in any other. In 1936 overwork and cardiac trouble finally proved too much for him. Chesterton died on 14 June, aged 62, too early to see fulfilled — at least in all the horror which between them Hitler and Stalin unleashed on the world — the prophecy he had made thirty years earlier. "the earnest Freethinkers", he wrote in 1906, "need not worry themselves so much about the persecutions of the past. Before the Liberal idea is dead or triumphant, we shall see wars and persecutions the like of which the world has never seen." Chesterton is buried in the Catholic cemetery in Beaconsfield, beneath a monument by the artist-craftsman Eric Gill. There are many epitaphs to him but Walter de la Mare's famous quatrain remains the justest as well as the most poignant:

> Knight of the Holy Ghost, he goes his way,
> Wisdom his motley, Truth his loving jest;
> The mills of Satan keep his lance in play,
> Pity and Innocence his heart at rest.

That just quoted gloomy prophecy of Chesterton's may itself be enough to dispel the image of him as a facile optimist; about most of the tendencies of his time he was anything but optimistic. Still, there are other images of him which can easily divert us from taking him seriously. Indeed, among the obstacles which stand in the way of our appreciating Chesterton's true greatness, the biggest perhaps is Chesterton himself. He readily lent himself to caricature and to the by now familiar picture of him as the jesting, bibulous journalist. The sight of his huge and rotund figure alighting from a hansom cab into Fleet Street was in itself enough to excite wonder among his contemporaries. But it was a sight rendered even more wonderful by the addition of certain accoutrements which seemed consciously designed to exaggerate a number of their possessor's natural characteristics; of these the most notable were, first, the heavy, black cape which had the effect, not of cloaking, but of showing off Chesterton's great girth, next, the crumpled sombrero which made him appear even taller than, at nearly six foot six, he already was, and, last, the silver sword-stick which only served to point up, a trifle superfluously one may now think, its owner's combative nature. Add to this larger than life figure the writer's playful style, and the personality quite dwarfs the thinker. We find it difficult to believe that such a lighthearted and dexterous style can be a vehicle for serious thought, let alone for exploring the ultimate questions; and this despite the fact that Chesterton regarded paradox for the sake of paradox as "contemptible". No more than Johnson's use of antithesis was Chesterton's of paradox an artistic pose or affectation; on the contrary, it was central to his world view.

There is another way of avoiding what is important about Chesterton and that is by situating him in the Edwardian period into whose political and moral controversies he entered with such zest, or as his critics would say, such mistaken zeal. Too many great Englishmen — Dr Johnson, whom in so many respects Chesterton resembled, again springs to mind as an obvious example — have been so assimilated to their own age that they no longer make any serious claims upon ours. We admit them into our minds, if at all, as objects rather of curiosity or mere antiquarian interest than as teachers whose words just might have an effect, even a profound effect, upon our own characters and modes of behaviour.

"It is the function ... of literature," Chesterton once wrote, to which one might add immodestly that it is the function even of so minor a work of literature as this, "to liberate a subject, or a spirit, or an incident, or a personality, from those irrelevancies which prevent it, first from being itself, and, secondly, from becoming perfectly allegorical of the essence of things. Everything about the cow in our daily experience of it which accidentally prevents us from realising its deeper magic, such, for instance, as our happening to be an old lady and afraid of cows, or our being an impecunious farmer and obliged to sell the cow, or even (though this is less likely) an ox and obliged to regard the cow with more specialised and perhaps more passionate sentiment — anything, I say, in the brute details of life, which hampers the particular sentiment we wish to regard her with, must in literature be eliminated ... we must put her in a book where her rounded cowishness will be safe from impertinences and side issues, from bulls who regard her as a female, and farmers who regard her as a property — and old ladies who regard her as the devil. Similar methods, I need hardly say, are needed to preserve the rounded humanity of the Cabinet Minister" (B 53-61, B 114-125).

It is the "rounded humanity" of Chesterton I am here concerned to "liberate". Which means that in the pages that follow little more will be seen of either the Fleet Street Character or the amiable historical specimen whose views, it is implied, are manifestly of a time but not for our time. There is no easier way of avoiding what to moderns are the uncomfortable and embarrassing aspects of Chesterton than by demonstrating, to one's own satisfaction at least, their eccentricity or historicity. We must try and see Chesterton, then, as he thought man must be seen: "against the sky".

But granted we will only see Chesterton 'in the round' — as alive for us, in other words — if we refuse to view him through the distorting lenses of either the caricaturist or the historicist, we must beware of flying from one error, which is after all a very human error, that of a warm partiality, only to find ourselves embracing another, which is a very inhuman error, that of a cold impartiality. For we would be less than faithful to the original if, in our eagerness to leave behind everything in Chesterton that we thought was accidental, the better to get at what we believe was essential, we ended up, not with any kind of realistic, flesh and blood picture of him, but with something altogether impersonal and incorporeal, akin to one of those impressionist canvases which Chesterton thought expressed a wilful subjectivity.

Chesterton above all believed in things, that is to say, concrete, individualised beings, whose essence is inextricably bound up with their existence. It may take us a while to see the "cowness" of that cow, as a consequence of our partial perspectives, but that doesn't at all mean that its cowness is a disembodied thing and apart from its being a cow. Chesterton believed that we get at the truth of a thing, not by abstracting from its thingness, but by paying due reverence and regard to it. It is the thingness of things, their being there, which is the miracle for which humankind should never cease to offer up thanks. Chesterton would have precisely reversed the terms of Descartes's "I think, therefore I am" to "I am, therefore I think". No doubt we do often see through a glass darkly, so that things are not always what they seem. But we should not, on that account, airily disdain the real:

> Whenever you hear much of things being unutterable and indefinable and impalpable and unnameable and subtly indescribable, then elevate your aristocratic nose towards heaven and snuff up the smell of decay. It is perfectly true that there is something in all good things that is beyond all speech or figure of speech. But it is also true that there is in all good things a perpetual desire for expression and concrete embodiment; and though the attempt to embody is always inadequate, the attempt is always made. If the idea does not seek to be the word, the chances are that it is an evil idea. If the word is not made flesh, it is a bad word .... The man who really thinks he has an idea will always try to explain that idea. The charlatan who has no idea will always confine himself to explaining that it is much too subtle to be explained. (C 30).

People who lay great stress on the mental, Chesterton thought, are quite likely to go mental, for want of the sustaining sanity which comes from the deliverances of our senses. In the grip of purely rationalist presuppositions, we first distort reality and finally despise it. "The truth is", wrote Chesterton, "that the modern world has had a mental breakdown more than a moral breakdown." Now whatever else Chesterton was, first and foremost he was a journalist, and this fact alone ensured that his mind (to whatever fancies it was prone) fed always on reality. Yet those in search of the 'essential' Chesterton have often wondered at the prodigality of a talent so fecklessly employed on trivial pieces — essays on 'everything'. But it was part of Chesterton's catholicism, with a small 'c', that 'everything' was grist to his journalistic mill. It was part of his ebullience and breadth of mind that he could be witty and eloquent on such an immense variety of subjects, many of them trivial, it's true, but in Chesterton's hands laced with truths that were far from trivial: *Tremendous Trifles*, as one of his collections of essays terms them. The fact is, that journalism was the element in which Chesterton's relish for the real found its outlet, and in which his characteristic genius for aphoristic utterance most shone. No doubt there were times when it seemed a treadmill or when work was undertaken out of a sense of duty, as when Chesterton took over the editorship of his brother's paper, the *New Witness*. But on the whole one has the impression that Chesterton got a great deal more pleasure than pain out of the literally thousands of pieces in which, with a "divine frivolity", he propounded his views.

I have said that Chesterton's vast output of journalistic essays, and anthologies of essays, is testimony to his realism as well as his universalism. And notwithstanding initial appearances to the contrary, this same interest in things — external, extra-mental things, existing out there in the real world — is also strongly present in his fictional writings. Here fantasy was the weapon Chesterton chose to defend reality, or to make more vivid and valuable to us those everyday, human things which we either take for granted or imagine, vainly, we can transcend.

The Napoleon of Notting Hill, published in 1904 and set eighty years later — in 1984 — opened with the choice of Auberon Quin as King of England. More as a practical joke than practical policy Quin conceives a scheme to restore the medieval boroughs, together with their old boundaries, offices and heraldic devices. Quin, whose very name suggests the quintessential aesthete, laments the loss of colour and variety from modern life. But his nostalgia is ineffectual and no match for what F R Leavis was later to call our "technologico-Benthamite civilization". It is the book's hero, Adam Wayne, an *homme sérieux*, who as provost of Notting Hill supplies the virtues of strength and determination which are lacking in Quin. He sets his face against the practical businessmen of the neighbouring boroughs whose plan for a new road would entail destroying one of Notting Hill's streets. Wayne's Notting Hill is also the small nation and the forces ranged against it the cosmopolitan empires envisaged by those, whether they be imperialists, international financiers or Fabian socialists, who for one reason or another are impatient to iron out mankind's differences. Near the start of the novel the reader is prepared for the book's controlling metaphor by a conversation which takes place between the exiled President of Nicaragua, whose country has lost its independence, and an English civil servant whose sympathies are all on the side of consolidation and uniformity.

"We moderns believe in a great cosmopolitan civilization, one which shall include all the talents of the absorbed peoples —"
"The Señor will forgive me," said the President.
"May I ask the Señor how, under ordinary circumstances, he catches a wild horse?"
"I never catch a wild horse," replied Barker, with dignity.
"Precisely," said the other; "and there ends your absorption of the talents. That is what I complain of in your cosmopolitanism. When you say you want all peoples to unite, you really mean that you want all peoples to unite to learn the tricks of your people. ... I recur to the example I gave. In Nicaragua we had a way of catching wild horses — by lassoing the fore feet - which was supposed to be the best in South America. If you are going to include all the talents, go and do it. If not, permit me to say what I have always said, that something went from the world when Nicaragua was civilised." (D, 40-41)

In *The Man Who Was Thursday*, to which novel Chesterton gave the subtitle of "A Nightmare", the central character, Gabriel Syme, finds himself enveloped in a cloud of Unreality, of indefinite shapes made up of dark and light, which he comes to recognize as resembling "the thing which the modern people call Impressionism, which is another name for that final scepticism which can find no floor to the universe" (E 127). But even in the midst of his bad dream Syme is reminded of the real:

He thought of all the human things in his story — of the Chinese lanterns in Saffron Park, of the girl's red hair in the garden, of the honest, beer-swilling sailors down by the dock, of his loyal companions standing by. Perhaps he had been chosen as a champion of all these fresh and kindly things to cross swords with the enemy of all creation. (E 118).

In all Chesterton's writings we find this championship of "human ... fresh and kindly things". To whatever nonsensical or fantastical or indeed mystical heights his imagination soared, his feet always remained firmly planted on the ground.

... And this high pride in being human had lifted him unaccountably to an infinite height above the monstrous men around him. For an instant, at least, he looked down upon all their sprawling eccentricities from the starry pinnacle of the commonplace. (E 66)

The "eccentricities" to which Chesterton here alludes were those he encountered in his art school days at The Slade, and *The Man Who Was Thursday* describes the nightmarish pessimism of his youth and how in the end daylight breaks in upon it to restore psychological and moral sanity. The novel's dedicatory poem to E C Bentley illuminates this personal allegory:

A cloud was on the mind of men
And wailing went the weather,
Yea, a sick cloud upon the soul
When we were boys together.
Science announced nonentity
And art admired decay;
The world was old and ended:
But you and I were gay;
Round us in antic order
Crippled vices came —
Lust that had lost its laughter,
Fear that had lost its shame.
Like the white lock of Whistler,
That lit our aimless gloom,
Men showed their own white feather

As proudly as a plume.
Life was a fly that faded,
And death a drone that stung;
The world was very old indeed
When you and I were young.

This is a tale of those old fears,
Even of those emptied hells,
And none but you shall understand
The true thing that it tells —
Of what colossal gods of shame
Could cow men and yet crash
Of what huge devils hid the stars,
Yet fell at a pistol flash.
The doubts that were so plain to chase,
So dreadful to withstand —
Oh, who shall understand but you;
Yes, who shall understand?
The doubts that drove us through the night
As we two walked amain,
And day had broken on the streets
Ere it broke upon the brain.
Between us, by the peace of God,
Such truth can now be told;
Yes, there is strength in striking root,
And good in growing old.
We have found common things at last,
And marriage and a creed,
And I may safely write it now,
And you may safely read. (E 5-7)

His mood of adolescent nihilism behind him, Chesterton never afterwards closed his eyes, Buddha-like, to the world or mistook it for mere flux. That way lies the road of Indifference which can end in criminal irresponsibility:

I've scarcely ever met a criminal who philosophized at all, who didn't philosophize along those lines of orientalism and recurrence and reincarnation, and the wheel of destiny and the serpent biting his own tail. (F 144)

There is a sense in which Chesterton's life was one long love affair with the world:

> If the arms of a man could be a fiery circle
> embracing the round world,
> I think I should be that man. (G 57)

Chesterton never lost his appetite, as so many in this century have done — preferring their own gnostic utopias — for the Good Things which the Creation pours all about us.

We can now see why Chesterton the man was of a piece with Chesterton's view of man. There is a sanity and wholeness in the one which we readily find in the other. In Chesterton there is no trace of that "dissociated sensibility" which T S Eliot saw as symptomatic of the modern condition. Chesterton resisted, quite consciously, the splitting apart of reason and emotion, mind and body, spirit and matter, which had occurred unconsciously in so many of his contemporaries. How had it occurred? The Victorian compromise, which culminated in the *fin-de-siècle,* and saw spiritualists quarrelling with scientific materialists, aesthetes with philistines, hedonists with puritans, was really the coming-home-to-roost of chickens which had been hatched some two centuries before. The disenchanted character of a world devoid of all 'secondary qualities' — sounds, tastes, colours and smells, not to mention a sense of value and purpose — had the inevitable effect of driving many to seek solace and meaning within the privacy of their own minds. Thus have some modern artists and thinkers travelled from romanticism and idealism to nihilism and solipsism. Others have gone the other way, succumbing to a reductionist view of man as simply a sophisticated piece of matter in motion: a creature differing in degree but not in kind from the other species which, like itself, are subject to inexorable physical laws. Chesterton battled against both kinds of heresy: the spiritualist and the materialist. He wanted, as it were, to put modern man back together again. But what made him singular among modern writers was the fact that he himself exemplified this 'togetherness' in his own person. He kept an undissociated sensibility while all about were losing, or had lost, or had never gained, theirs. Everything about Chesterton, most notably of course his religion, tended towards the incarnational.

2. The Heresy — and Heresies — of Modernity

Most biographers of Chesterton, in an effort one supposes to encompass every last colourful detail of his life as well as to make him more accessible (and amiable) to a contemporary audience, have found neither the space nor the inclination to connect the inner life with the outer. They have consequently glossed over or underplayed the extent to which Chesterton was at war with the modern world. We read of his lively engagements, on public platforms as well as in print, with the likes of Wells, Shaw and Kipling. But missing so often from such accounts is any sense either that Chesterton's jousts were more than merely jests or that his criticisms could as well be made today — and are of equal relevance today — as when he first uttered them.

Many of the fashionable ideas against which Chesterton pitted his eloquence no doubt seem as strange to us now as the social landscape they once aspired to alter or influence. But there is one idea - underlying all the others — which is as familiar today as it was in Chesterton's time. This is the utilitarian idea that social problems are best tackled by dwelling not on their causes but on their consequences. We still habitually focus, as Chesterton's contemporaries also did, on the dire effects of alcoholism or drug abuse or divorce or sexual promiscuity, with a view to demonstrating why such 'unprofitable' behaviour is best avoided. But in so far as we moderns obey injunctions of the 'thou shalt not' sort it is without any sense that the sum of our negations might amount to a morally justified or meaningful life. We avoid evil essentially in order to avoid pain, not out of any positive desire to do good by ourselves or others. As Chesterton put it, "... only the knowledge of evil remains to us .... A modern morality ... can only point with absolute

conviction to the horrors that follow breaches of law; its only
certainty is a certainty of ill. It can only point to imperfection. It has
no perfection to point to." (H 24, 17)

This supping upon horrors, it may be urged, is for our own good.
But as a prophylactic against evil it is surely not preferable to the
contemplation of the Good, the True and the Beautiful. "A young
man may keep himself from vice by continually thinking of disease.
He may keep himself from it also by continually thinking of the
Virgin Mary. There may be question about which method is the
more reasonable, or even about which is the more efficient. But
surely there can be no question about which is the more whole-
some." (H 19) What Chesterton called the "negative spirit" of
modernity is not simply unwholesome, either; it is also ineffectual
in its own terms: as a means of warding off evil. Plato's 'care of the
soul', practised by individuals strongly imbued from an early age
with an idea of the good life, was a kind of preventive moral
medicine, whereas what has replaced it — Bentham's 'felicific
calculus' — only begins to take effect once we have actually
perceived or experienced the painful consequences of certain types
of behaviour. As a result, we really only deal with problems when
it is too late to deal with them; when, so to speak, people are already
well down the slippery slope to ruin and oblivion. It never seems to
occur to us that our proliferating personal and social disorders are the
price we pay for jettisoning — or failing to inculcate — the
knowledge of Good. So long as the amendment of modern lives and
laws has always to wait upon our experience of moral disorder, and
the distress it causes, so long will we find ourselves devoting more
and more of our resources to the hospitals and social services, to the
police, prisons and rehabilitation centres. We are inhibited by our
liberal outlook from getting to the root of the problem, precisely
because our liberal outlook is the problem. Liberalism, in its heyday
in the nineteenth century, claimed to have rendered obsolete the old
creeds: man had 'come of age' and could live perfectly well without
them. And for a time he did, for even after the Christian religion had
departed from a person's life the restraints and responsibilities it had

taught him remained, in the attenuated form, for example, of that 'middle class respectability' which Chesterton's parents, unbelievers both, clung to in common with so many others of their generation. Such respectability has been a long time dying, but Chesterton saw that it could not continue indefinitely in "the absence of vivid pictures of purity and spiritual triumph" (H 20), of the kind which for centuries had shaped the mind and spirit of Western man.

> A great silent collapse, an enormous unspoken disappointment, has in our time fallen on our Northern civilization. All previous ages have sweated and been crucified, in an attempt to realize what is really the right life, what was really the good man. A definite part of the modern world has come beyond question to the conclusion that there is no answer to these questions, that the most that we can do is to set up a few notice-boards at places of obvious danger, to warn men, for instance, against drinking themselves to death, or ignoring the mere existence of their neighbours. Ibsen is the first to return from the baffled hunt to bring us the tidings of great failure.
>
> Every one of the popular modern phrases and ideals is a dodge in order to shirk the problem of what is good. We are fond of talking about 'liberty'; that, as we talk of it, is a dodge to avoid discussing what is good. We are fond of talking about 'progress'; that is a dodge to avoid discussing what is good. We are fond of talking about 'education'; that is a dodge to avoid discussing what is good. The modern man says, "Let us leave all these arbitrary standards and embrace liberty." That is, logically rendered, "Let us not decide what is good, but let it be considered good not to decide it." He says, "Away with your old moral formulae; I am for progress." This, logically stated, means, "Let us not settle what is good; but let us settle whether we are getting more of it." He says, "Neither in religion nor morality, my friend, lie the hopes of the race, but in education." This, clearly expressed, means, "We cannot decide what is good, but let us give it to our children." (H 24-26)

It would not be quite accurate to say that in place of the Good which once (however imperfectly) governed men's lives in Western society, modern man has put nothing at all. Nihilism, or its sanitised equivalent — the social engineer's Olympian neutrality — there certainly is; as a society we are less and less sure of what if anything unites us. But although on a public level the Good has been replaced by the Useful, and indeed can only be taken seriously on this level when construed as Useful, on another level, that of people's private lives, the Good has been dissolved into a mass of different and mutually competing goods. The modern in search of a morally satisfying system is spoilt for choice, just as he is in the 'shopping mall' or supermarket. But whatever morality a person chooses, it becomes his 'personal morality'; and more than whether it is right what matters is the fact that it is his. Or to put it slightly differently, a belief in one's self is more important than a belief in something external to one's self; the latter being acceptable only in so far as it is reducible to the former. "I believe in myself," is the proudest motto of the modern. Chesterton thought that anyone who really "believes in himself" is on the way to becoming either a rotter or a lunatic. Complete self-confidence by definition excludes so much else in life which is necessary and valuable that it ends inevitably in a kind of solipsism which is not just bad but mad. And when, moreover, the man who believes in himself finds, to his utter dismay, that the self he has erected into a god has failed him, his natural recourse is to suicide.

When, in response to a point of view advanced by another, a person says, "I buy that," the expression is testimony at once to the privatisation and the commercialisation of morality. We no longer take seriously theories or cosmic philosophies in the sense of thinking they will have any real or measurable effect on our world. But in a plural and relativistic society we do take very seriously every person's right to hold such a theory or philosophy. We consequently flout the canons of modern good taste if we trespass too far on a man's personal morality by attempting to intrude our own. But when we do so it is the claims of subjectivity not of truth which we are accused of denying. As well-adjusted moderns we are meant to regard with a kind of equanimity the variety of views we encounter.

... there is one thing that is infinitely more absurd and unpractical than burning a man for his philosophy. This is the habit of saying that his philosophy does not matter, and this is done universally in the twentieth century .... A man's opinion on tramcars matters; his opinion on Botticelli matters; his opinion on all things does not matter. He may turn over and explore a million objects, but he must not find that strange object, the universe; for if he does he will have a religion, and be lost. Everything matters - except everything ... (H 4-5)

Chesterton, of course, thought that theories matter very much, as this passage clearly shows. But how does one explain that to someone for whom moral theories are purely matters of personal taste, and hence of no more consequence than a liking for smoked salmon or Liberty fabrics? One might begin by pointing out that this reduction of morality to the realm of the personal is itself a theory and, as such, no less fraught with consequences than any other theory. By it we imply that our ideas are right in the same way that the clothes we wear are right, if they suit us; and if they don't we discard them. Now it is in the very nature of morality that it is only with difficulty 'made to measure' for each individual; the opposite is more nearly the case: an individual has to measure up to a morality, adjusting himself to it rather than expecting it to adjust itself to him. A 'personal morality', at least in the sense in which that term is now usually understood, is an oxymoron. Worse, it is a synonym for every sort of half-truth which, as it were, has been pressed into personal service as the whole truth. The Truth is simply too large a garment for modern man to 'wear'; he can only be comfortable with fragments of it. Thus the bit we choose — our 'personal morality' — is not immorality; but it is inevitably sectarian or narrow: a part of the truth which unfortunately we mistake for the whole.

The modern world is not evil; in some ways the modern world is far too good. It is full of wild and wasted virtues. When a religious scheme is shattered (as Christianity was shattered at the Reformation), it is not merely the vices that are let loose. The vices are, indeed, let loose, and they wander and do damage. But the virtues are let loose also; and the virtues wander more wildly, and the virtues do more

terrible damage. The modern world is full of the old Christian virtues
gone mad. The virtues have gone mad because they have been
isolated from each other and are wandering alone ...

... There is a huge and heroic sanity of which moderns can only
collect the fragments. There is a giant of whom we see only the lopped
arms and legs walking about. They have torn the soul of Christ into
silly strips, labelled egoism and altruism, and they are equally puzzled
by His insane magnificence and His insane meekness. They have
parted His garments among them, and for His vesture they have cast
lots; though the coat was without seam woven from the top throughout.
(I 38-9, 65)

The modern world is thus peopled with individuals each clinging,
when they are still clinging to anything at all, to the remnants of a
moral system whose original unity they have carelessly rent asun-
der. Men pique themselves on being 'heretics' without realising that
this means they are monomaniacs. They are Dostoyevsky's "terrible *simplificateurs*", unbalanced in their one-sided moral attachments. There is also no arguing with them, for they have perfectly
good logical arguments for their arbitrary positions. Like the
madman who imagines he's Napoleon they are unshakeable in their
convictions.

If you argue with a madman, it is extremely probable that you will get
the worst of it; for in many ways his mind moves all the quicker for
not being delayed by the things that go with good judgment. He is
not hampered by a sense of humour or by charity, or by the dumb
certainties of experience. He is the more logical for losing certain
sane affections. Indeed, the common phrase for insanity is in this
respect a misleading one. The madman is not the man who has lost
his reason. The madman is the man who has lost everything except
his reason. (I 18-19)

The modern heretic (one who arbitrarily chooses) is as easily
spotted as the old, by his insane belief in the omniscience of
whatever ideas he has made his own. Take the materialist. He is not
wrong, as the idealist thinks him, to place a value on the material
components of our nature. He is wrong to place an absolute value

on them. He is wrong, first, because his explanation is not adequate to the reality it describes; it is too simple: it does not so much explain things as explain them away.

> The Christian is quite free to believe that there is a considerable amount of settled order and inevitable development in the universe. But the materialist is not allowed to admit into his spotless machine the slightest speck of spiritualism or miracle .... The Christian admits that the universe is manifold and even miscellaneous, just as a sane man knows that he is complex. The sane man knows that he has a touch of the best, a touch of the devil, a touch of the saint, a touch of the citizen. Nay, the really sane man knows that he has a touch of the madman. But the materialist's world is quite simple and solid, just as the madman is quite sure he is sane. (I 28)

There are many different species of materialist and some of them can seem quite benign at first glance. There is, for example, the type which tells us that we cannot help our misdemeanours and crimes. We are not responsible for them; our heredity or environment is. There is thus no use anyone appealing to our better selves or bidding us to 'sin no more'. From this view of man as a helpless victim of his conditioning there flows the inhuman vision of a society ruled over by the conditioners. Through techniques of positive reinforcement perfected in the laboratory by behaviourial scientists an environment can be created in which men, no less than rats, will behave properly, or rationally. Another group of materialists, called eugenicists in Chesterton's day, genetic engineers in our own, share with behaviourists the assumption that human beings are irresponsible; only in their case they want to operate on us before birth rather than after it. The trouble is, of course, that the eugenicist, like the behaviourist, and in fact like all materialists, must make himself an exception to his own rule: you are determined, they are determined, I am the determiner (or conditioner). If all human beings are 'victims' of their environment or heredity, so too are behaviourists and eugenicists (assuming them also to be human!) On the materialist's hypothesis, the materialist's mentality is no less determined by circumstances outside his control than the spiritualist's.

Upon what right, then, if even his own theory denies him one, does the behaviourial or genetic engineer rest his claim to re-shape the rest of us? The answer, of course, is the old gnostic one: it is the claim to a special or superior knowledge to which only a small elite is privy. When we can no longer clearly agree upon what is normal or abnormal, when we have begun to doubt the great common (and commonsensical) ideas which once united us, then the way is open for the specialist to enforce his own conception of health or happiness. Unless we keep a firm grip on "the public and accepted meaning of life or safety or prosperity or pleasure", we may easily fall into the hands of specialists who have their own peculiar definitions of what constitutes our good.

> Now, that specialists are valuable for this particular and practical purpose, of predicting the approach of enormous and admitted human calamities, nobody but a fool would deny. But that does not bring us one inch nearer to allowing them the right to define what is a calamity; or to call things calamities which common sense does not call calamities. We call in the doctor to save us from death; and, in death being admittedly an evil, he has the right to administer the queerest and most recondite pill which he may think is a cure for all such menaces of death. He has not the right to administer death, as the cure for all human ills. And as he has no moral authority to enforce a new conception of happiness, so he has no moral authority to enforce a new conception of sanity. (J 47)

What warrant exists for believing a particular materialist viewpoint, be it behaviourist or geneticist, Marxist or Freudian, is said to derive from the workings of the cosmos whose laws a man can no more escape than he can jump out of his own skin. In fact, this unchallengeable appearance of scientific objectivity is somewhat misleading, since such theories are more truly the product of a self-sufficient reason than of disinterested empirical observation. Indeed only a rationalist, with nothing but cogitation to go on, could seriously maintain that everything is reducible to matter. The materialist conceals, as much from himself perhaps as the rest of us, the fact that his theory really began in himself. Still, he at least pays homage to the created world, even if the picture he has formed of it errs towards the mundane.

By contrast, the idealist really does believe that everything begins in himself. He celebrates without embarrassment the self's creativity, distrusting altogether the deliverances of his own senses. This other extreme of modern speculation is quite literally mental. The materialist, for example through the utilitarian test of pleasure or the pragmatic test of 'what works', at least retains some tenuous grip on the external world, albeit a world shrunk to the proportions of a narrow, rationalist theory. But the idealist, recoiling from modern reason because of the evidently crippling effect it has had upon man, abandons all pretence of realism. Instead, he declares that man's 'unconquerable will' is what matters and not any low considerations of human happiness. So not only does the idealist attack the materialist's standard of happiness or pleasure as a proper reason for a man's actions, he equally attacks all external standards, admitting only the will as a test of right action.

> But you cannot praise an action because it shows will; for to say that is merely to say that it is an action. By this praise of will you cannot really choose one course as better than another. And yet choosing one course as better than another is the very definition of the will you are praising.
> The worship of will is the negation of will. To admire mere choice is to refuse to choose. (I 55)

Materialists and idealists alike are to be found in the ranks of the futurists, or modern utopians. This is hardly surprising since there is little 'future' for their ideas in the present, and what support there might have been for them in the past can only be suggested by the most selective readings of history. The present and the past, the visionary fanatic is usually forced to admit, are characterised by all kinds of intolerance or, in other words, by a failure to accommodate egalitarianism or feminism or vegetarianism, or what have you. The future, on the other hand, exhibits no such recalcitrant attitudes; it is blissfully 'open'. This 'openness' is exhilarating and explains much of the utopian's appeal. But it is also an accessory to the utopian's own unacknowledged intolerance. Precisely because the future is a blank slate upon which, unhindered, the utopian imagines he can write anything he wishes, it is an invitation and an incitement to the narrow mind. All the richness and complexity of reality falls away in the fantasy of a future made safe for one simple, dominating idea. Anything's possible, or can seem so, if you live, so to speak, in the future. The future is frontier-land and the trick is to get there first and stake out your claim to it. The inhumanity of the utopian, so tragically enacted in our century, springs from the conjunction between a limited vision and an unlimited opportunity; the latter is conjured up in thought by 'the future' and in practice by a particular set of circumstances of the kind which obtained in Russia in 1917, in Germany in 1933 and in Cambodia in 1975.

Chesterton charged the utopians of his time with a failure to see "that the thing which is valuable and lovable in our eyes is man - the old beer-drinking, creed-making, fighting, failing, sensual, respectable man." (H 60) Speaking of H G Wells's narrow scientific outlook Chesterton summarised the weakness of all utopian schemes, then and since:

> ... that they take the greatest difficulty of man and assume it to be overcome, and then give an elaborate account of the overcoming of the smaller ones. (H 73)

So far we have been discussing the narrow dogmas of modern materialists and idealists. However, it must be admitted that, mercifully, none of them has exactly triumphed in that part of the world which we may still be permitted to call Western civilization. Granted that there abounds in these societies a bewildering variety of single-idea fanatics, many of whom would dearly like to get their hands on the levers of power. But the idea, if idea it can be called, which reigns supreme in contemporary Western society is much vaguer than any of those we have so far been studying. It is the idea of 'progress' which, chameleon-like, can taken on the colour of other ideas while remaining distinct from them. Chesterton

objected to the modernist dogmas of his day not because they were
dogmas, but because they were wrong. He objected to the idea of
progress because, in its eschewal of all dogmas, it could not properly
define itself: how can one say what progress truly is if there exists
no clear idea either of what one is progressing away from or what one
is progressing towards? The progressive fondly imagines that ideas,
like consumer goods, can safely be left to find their true value in a
competitive market-place, or like animal species to struggle for
survival in an evolutionary process from which, it is blithely
assumed, the fittest will inevitably emerge victorious. A society
such as ours which is under the sway of the idea of progress is
perpetually putting off the question of what is ultimately good or in
what the good life for a man might consist.

> The case of the general talk of "progress" is, indeed, an extreme one.
> As enunciated to-day, "progress" is simply a comparative of which we
> have not settled the superlative. We meet every ideal of religion,
> patriotism, beauty, or brute pleasure with the alternative ideal of
> progress - that is to say, we meet every proposal of getting something
> that we know about, with an alternative proposal of getting a great deal
> more of nobody knows what. Progress, properly understood, has,
> indeed, a most dignified and legitimate meaning. But as used in
> opposition to precise moral ideals, it is ludicrous. So far from it being
> the truth that the ideal of progress is to be set against that of ethical
> or religious finality, the reverse is the truth. Nobody has any business
> to use the word "progress" unless he has a definite creed and a cast-
> iron code of morals. Nobody can be progressive without being
> doctrinal; I might almost say that nobody can be progressive without
> being infallible - at any rate, without believing in some infallibility.
> For progress by its very name indicates a direction; and the moment
> we are in the least doubtful about the direction, we become in the same
> degree doubtful about the progress. Never perhaps since the beginning
> of the world has there been an age that had less right to use the word
> "progress" than we. (H 27-8)

To the Chestertonian critique of progress the liberal might with
justice reply that the word "progress" does mean something to each
individual, for the simple reason that each individual has his own

idea of the good and so can tell whether or not he is advancing towards it. This might be true if the relativism of our age did not imply, as self-evidently it does, that every idea of the good bears a conditional and not an unconditional character. Our ceaseless chatter about 'values' betrays the pass to which our progress has brought us. We are not sure that the values we embrace sincerely today we won't shrug off just as sincerely tomorrow. Every moral good is, then, a contingent good: contingent upon the present stage of man's evolution, or upon our class and upbringing, or upon the kind of 'life style' to which our personality is temporarily drawn.

This moral pluralism, far from being a liberating force, goes a long way towards explaining the mindless conformity and passivity of modern Western societies. It chains each one of us ever more securely to the mechanical and aimless processes of production and consumption.

> The more the life of the mind is unhinged, the more the machinery of matter will be left to itself ... the man we see every day - the worker in Mr Gradgrind's factory, the little clerk in Mr Gradgrind's office — he is too mentally worried to believe in freedom. He is kept quiet with revolutionary literature. He is calmed and kept in his place by a constant succession of wild philosophies. He is a Marxian one day, a Nietzscheite the next day, a Superman (probably) the next day; and a slave every day. (I 179-80)

We shall have more to say of Chesterton's critique of progressive civilization in later chapters. Suffice it to say here that Chesterton saw our much vaunted progress away from the traditional religion and philosophy of the West as indicating a visible decline: from a more to a less human way of life.

> Man can hardly be defined, after the fashion of Carlyle, as an animal who makes tools; ants and beavers and many other animals make tools, in the sense that they make an apparatus. Man can be defined as an animal that makes dogmas. As he piles doctrine on doctrine and conclusion on conclusion in the formation of some tremendous scheme of philosophy and religion, he is, in the only legitimate sense

of which the expression is capable, becoming more and more human. When he drops one doctrine after another in a refined scepticism, when he declines to tie himself to a system, when he says that he has outgrown definitions, when he says that he disbelieves in finality, when, in his own imagination, he sits as God, holding no form of creed but contemplating all, then he is by that very process sinking slowly backwards into the vagueness of the vagrant animals and the unconsciousness of the grass. Trees have no dogmas. Turnips are singularly broad-minded. (H 288-9)

Chesterton had at least this much to say for most of the writers whose views he opposed, namely that they had definite convictions. He simply held that they were dogmatic and wrong while he was dogmatic and right. But the real enemy of civilization is the moral neutral who asks, with Pilate, "What is truth?" For Chesterton the question is not merely rhetorical; it demands an answer.

The vice of the modern notion of mental progress is that it is always something concerned with the breaking of bonds, the effacing of boundaries, the casting away of dogmas. But if there be such a thing as mental growth, it must mean the growth into more and more definite convictions, into more and more dogmas. The human brain is a machine for coming to conclusions (H 287-8)

We must now turn to the conclusions Chesterton himself came to, and the definite philosophy of life which he opposed to the heresies of modernity.

3. Christian Orthodoxy

To say that the modern world is rotten with materialism is to run no great risk of contradiction. Indeed the remark has attained the status almost of a truism, so that even the most complacently prosperous among us will be hard put to deny it. But to say that the modern world is rotten with spiritualism, or idealism, would almost certainly provoke expressions of outright shock and disagreement. And yet Chesterton was always more disturbed by the doubts of the spiritualists — "the last and worst doubts" — than the doubts of the materialists. At least the latter accept the earth, in which sense they are nearer to heaven than the former who imagine they made it.

The modern project to master the world, to become, as Descartes put it, *les maîtres et possesseurs de nature,* has been an idealist project. It sprang from an idealisation of man's mind at the expense of matter; from a belief in the omniscience of the one and the nescience of the other. Nature, in the modern estimation of it, has lost all its former traces of divinity, ceasing altogether to be the handiwork of God — His creation — and becoming instead a lifeless thing, devoid of all goodness and value. In so far as God is still thought to exist at all, it is as a distant, aloof being, far removed from the workings of the world and its physical laws.

It is not too fanciful to see something Manichaean behind the drive of modern technological man to dominate nature. To the ancient Manichaeans, and the medieval sects — Catharists and Albigensians — descended from them, this world is the creation not of God on high, but of a lower spirit, a malign demiurge. In a not dissimilar fashion, moderns see the external world as indifferent or even hostile to human purposes. In both Manichaeanism and its modern, secular counterparts there is also the same belief that man can somehow make himself independent of nature. Imprisoned within the worthless clay of man's animal nature, so the old Manichaeans believed, there is a 'divine spark', with the aid of which we can escape the evils of this world by developing a direct knowledge or *gnosis* of God. The old Manichaean sects thus fed on the pains and humiliations of socially disaffected groups of people, to whom, however, they could offer little more by way of consolation than this esoteric theology of hope. But in modern times the theology has become, simultaneously, an ideology and a technology. All of us are influenced in some degree by the gnostic idea, now variously disguised as Progress or Evolution or Historical Inevitability, that an originally intractable nature, including human nature, can be transcended and a world then created more amenable to our heart's desires. The harm comes not from the purely material blessings of our technological culture, but from the rationalist, née Manichaean, spirit of pride and conquest in which it is rooted.

It is the spirit that would liberate us from 'the bondage of vice and virtue'; in order words from original sin. The old Manichaean sects were said to exhibit extremes of both asceticism and sensualism. Both attitudes were possible to a person who held the body in contempt: either one shrunk from its touch or grossly violated it, but in neither posture could one be accused of treating it as a sacred vessel. It is not so different with us. In one mood we hold ourselves proudly aloof from our corporeal nature, or the clockwork of matter that it has become for us, inventing our own standards of value without reference to a natural law which, if it exists at all, seems not to concern us. In another mood we act as beings wholly determined by our natural impulses, with no motives other than those bequeathed to us by our genes. In practice, modern man flits between the life of an autonomous being to which he is urged by idealists and the life of an automaton to which he is condemned by materialists. It seems we must either abandon this world altogether, in favour of a better, or abandon ourselves *to* it, in lieu of a better. World-weariness and worldliness have at least this much in common, that they leave one equally bereft of the capacity to appreciate things; with the result that we tend to regard the gifts of creation with despair or presumption. Chesterton recalled the pessimists of his boyhood, who, when confronted with the dandelion, said with Swinburne:

> I am weary with days and hours
> Blown buds of barren flowers,
> Desires and dreams and powers
> And everything but sleep.

> But there is a way of despising the dandelion which is not that of the dreary pessimist, but of the more offensive optimist ... ultimately based on the strange and staggering heresy that a humanbeing has a *right* to dandelions; that in some extraordinary fashion we can demand the very pick of all the dandelions in the garden of Paradise; that we owe no thanks for them at all and need feel no wonder at them at all; and above all no wonder at being thought worthy to receive them. Instead of saying, like the old religious poet, 'What is man that Thou carest for him, or the son of man that Thou regardest him?' we are to say like the discontented cabman, 'What's this?' or like the bad-tempered Major in the club, 'Is this a chop fit for a gentleman?' Now I not only dislike this attitude quite as much as the Swinburnian pessimistic attitude, but I think it comes to very much the same thing; to the actual loss of appetite for the chop or the dish of dandelion-tea. And the name of it is Presumption and the name of its twin brother is Despair. (A 305-6)

There is a typically Chestertonian paradox in modern man's sense of alienation from the mechanical world he has created. For it is as a consequence of the world being too much with him, too much a projection of his own disembodied mind, that the modern man now finds it such an alien and inhospitable place. From the over-valuation of man's reason has come the devaluation of nature. There is a loss of vision entailed in putting the mental cart before the material horse; for we then see the horse as 'no more' than a random instance of universal (and cart-like) laws of motion. In effect, this is to misplace the horse. Its intrinsic value and identity, what we might call its horse-ness, is lost to our view. It is so with the whole universe of things when they are seen instrumentally; which is to say, rationalistically. When the world is shrunk to the size and dimensions attributed to it by our rationalizing intellects, we get the measure of it, but at the price of losing the fullness of it. This would perhaps have done less damage if at the same time we had not also lost God. There was nothing in the remote figure of the 'Watchmaker' deity, who had originally wound up the world, to counterbalance our sense of being alone in a mindless and purposeless universe.

How, then, are we to recapture a sense, however fleetingly glimpsed, of the world's being and the fullness thereof? We might begin by exactly reversing the terms of the aforementioned paradox so that it yields a positive rather than a negative outcome. The benign paradox, which is central to so much of Chesterton's thinking, is this: that to gain the world — the real world — we must first lose it, by sundering it from the mind. Then we will find that though the world was perhaps made for us, it was not made by us. We will have entered what Chesterton called "the sunny country of common sense" (I 72) in which what strikes us as more wonderful than the fact that the world can be explained is the fact that it cannot be explained. To the rationalist, confined in the dark chamber of his mental processes, the world is what he thinks it is. There is no mystery to it: it is the product of certain discernible physical and biological laws. But of course it is nothing of the sort, as Chesterton well knew. It may be that one tree is so constituted chemically that it produces apples while another produces acorns, but this is only a more elaborate way of saying that apple trees produce apples and oak trees acorns. And the fact that they do so is not necessary; it is given. We could just as well imagine them producing something else, or nothing come to that. Chesterton admits that reason and necessity have their place in the scheme of things: "There are certain sequences of developments (cases of one thing following another), which are, in the true sense of the word, reasonable. They are, in the true sense of the word, necessary. Such are mathematical and merely logical sequences" (I 74). The mistake occurs when we use the rules of the mind to dictate to the things outside the mind. We talk "as if the fact that trees bear fruit were just as *necessary* as the fact that two and one trees make three. But it is not. There is an enormous difference by the test of fairyland; which is the test of the imagination. You cannot *imagine* two and one not making three. But you can easily imagine trees not growing fruit; you can imagine them growing golden candlesticks or tigers hanging on by the tail" (I 75). Trees stand and everything exists, if not by magic, then by a miracle; but not at any rate by sets of necessary laws which we import into them. We can now see why modern scientific man has taken the existence of things too much for granted; and why as a consequence their very existence is now threatened.

> Until we realize that things might not be, we cannot realize that things are. Until we see the background of darkness we cannot admire the light as a single and created things. As soon as we have seen that darkness, all light is lightning, sudden, blinding, and divine. Until we picture nonentity we underrate the victory of God, and can realize none of the trophies of His ancient war. It is one of the million wild jests of truth that we know nothing until we know nothing. (H 58-9)

Chesterton believed that in the life of St Francis of Assisi there had been enacted this same vision of the infinite value of everything when seen against the background of nothing.

> It is commonly in a somewhat cynical sense that men have said, "Blessed is he that expecteth nothing, for he shall not be disappointed." It was in a wholly happy and enthusiastic sense that St Francis said, "Blessed is he would expecteth nothing, for he shall enjoy everything." It was by this deliberate idea of starting from zero, from the dark nothingness of his own deserts, that he did come to enjoy even earthly things as few people have enjoyed them. (K 84-5)

We would value our world much more, as we would anything, if we regarded it as ours not by right but by luck; as not only a pleasure to be enjoyed carelessly but a privilege to be exercised carefully. Then, instead of the prodigal wastefulness we show towards things, we would feel for them "a sort of sacred thrift". (I 99)

I really felt (the fancy may seem foolish) as if all the order and number of things were the romantic remnant of Crusoe's ship. That there are two sexes and one sun, was like the fact that there were two guns and one axe. It was poignantly urgent that none should be lost; but somehow, it was rather fun that none could be added. The trees and the planets seemed like things saved from the wreck: and when I saw the Matterhorn I was glad that it had not been overlooked in the confusion. I felt economical about the stars as if they were sapphires (they are called so in Milton's Eden): I hoarded the hills. For the universe is a single jewel, and while it is a natural cant to talk of a jewel as peerless and priceless, of this jewel it is literally true. This cosmos is indeed without peer and without price: for there cannot be another one. (I 100-101)

A person's attitude towards the cosmos, Chesterton thought, should be like a patriot's towards his country. There is a primary loyalty and love long before there is any approval or disapproval. Love is not blind but it is bound. Men feel bound to a particular place or country by ties of allegiance which far outweigh any rational calculations of personal or mutual advantage. But this irrational devotion does not issue in stagnation or complacency. On the contrary, a loving attentiveness is characteristic of those who love a thing, not for a reason, but for itself; and who are all the more alive, therefore, to the corruptions which might befall a thing through neglect or some other cause. A gardener does not demonstrate his love for a tree by neglecting to prune it. Similarly, the wife who loves her husband is not always disposed to leave him as he is; it really is (as she claims) for his own good that in some ways she wants to change him. It is so also with the cosmic patriot: he loves the manifold forms in which being defines and expresses itself; but in guarding them against possible perversions he will be more like the active soldier than the passive contemplative. Chesterton believed that the "first loyalty to things" should act as a stimulant not a tranquillizer, evoking resolution not resignation. But it will do so only if a firm line is first drawn between the cosmic patriotism of Christianity and the cosmic pantheism of the old nature worshippers. Of the latter we may fondly recall only the innocent side:

nature bathed in the fresh light of morning, glowing with amiability. But what begins in an idolisation of nature's kindness ends in an imitation of her cruelty:

> Nature worship is natural enough while the society is young, or, in other words, Pantheism is all right as long as it is the worship of Pan. But Nature has another side which experience and sin are not slow in finding out, and it is no flippancy to say of the God Pan that he soon showed the cloven hoof. The only objection to Natural Religion is that somehow it always becomes unnatural. A man loves Nature in the morning for her innocence and amiability, and at nightfall, if he is loving her still, it is for her darkness and her cruelty. He washes in dawn in clear water as did the Wise Man of the Stoics, yet, somehow at the dark end of the day, he is bathing in hot bull's blood, as did Julian the Apostate. The mere pursuit of health always leads to something unhealthy. Physical nature must not be made the direct object of obedience; it must be enjoyed, not worshipped. Stars and mountains must not be taken seriously. If they are, we end where the pagan nature worship ended. Because the earth is kind, we can imitate all her cruelties. Because sexuality is sane, we can all go mad about sexuality. Mere optimism had reached its insane and appropriate termination. The theory that everything was good had become an orgy of everything that was bad. (I 123-4)

When the outer world loses all appearance of virtue, the virtuous seek consolation in the Inner Light. This was the position of the last Stoics, like Marcus Aurelius, whose doctrine was really a counsel of despair. They gave up on the world as beyond redemption and sought instead to cultivate a cold if courageous detachment. The dilemma of the ancients, of loving the world either too much or too little, is our dilemma, too. Chesterton thought that the answer to this cosmic dilemma, then as now, is the Christian answer. Reasoning by analogy from what experience teaches us, we can infer — as a probability if not a certainty — that the original, divine act of creation had at least something in common with all subsequent, human acts of creation, namely, that it was an act of separation. God is separate and distinct from His creation, the world, as the poet is from his poem or the mother from her new-born child. God is not immanent in all things, as the pantheist would have it, but transcendent and separate from the cosmos; not so transcendent, though, as to lose all interest in things after they have been created, as the deist or evolutionist would have it. The processes of Becoming neither obliterate nor explain, though they may make us forgetful of, the primordial fact of Being.

> This principle that all creation and procreation is a breaking off is at least as consistent through the cosmos as the evolutionary principle that all growth is a branching out. A woman loses a child even in having a child. All creation is separation. Birth is as solemn a parting as death. (I 126)

It follows from this prime principle of Christianity that in making the world, God set it free.

> In this way at least one could be both happy and indignant without degrading one's self to be either a pessimist or an optimist. On this system one could fight all the forces of existence without deserting the flag of existence. One could be at peace with the universe and yet be at war with the world. (I 126-7)

At first sight it might seem as though an Aristotelian ethics would follow naturally from this view of existence. There is certainly, in the Christian sense of balance, an avoidance of the extremes of optimism and pessimism: the world is neither to be worshipped nor despised. But the history of Christianity does not lend itself plausibly to the picture of it as a religion of mere moderation.

> There was really an element in it of emphasis and even frenzy which had justified the secularists in their superficial criticism. It might be wise, I began more and more to think that it was wise, but it was not merely worldly wise; it was not merely temperate and respectable. Its fierce crusaders and meek saints might balance each other; still, the crusaders were very fierce and the saints were very meek, meek beyond all decency. (I 150-51)

In Christianity, as in Christ Himself, the balance is held, not by diluting one's love or anger in the safe solution of compromise, but by giving each in turn its due weight when the occasion demands it. Rational calculation is not an adequate response either to the primal goodness or the subsequent perversions of existence. And it does not adequately explain our virtuous behaviour. Courage, for example, though in theory it can be made to seem the golden mean between recklessness and cowardice, in practice is more nearly "a contradiction in terms. It means a strong desire to live taking the form of a readiness to die. 'He that will lose his life, the same shall save it' .... This paradox is the whole principle of courage." (I 153)

Similarly, Christian modesty holds proper pride and humility in equal esteem; its virtue does not consist simply in a moderation made out of watering down the two. A mild rationalist modesty neither lifts the heart nor cleanses the soul. Better that men go barefoot in sackcloth and ashes or clad in raiment of crimson and gold than that they aspire to no more than a grey and sober-suited contentment. Better still if, like Thomas à Becket, they wear a hairshirt under their crimson and gold. "It is at least better than the manner of the modern millionaire, who has the black and the drab outwardly for others, and the gold next his heart." (I 165) Grey, that blurring of black and white, is precisely the anaemic hue which moral relativism brings to mind. Not so Christian ethics, which is a coat of many primary colours; it is anything but grey. It combines levity with gravity, so doing justice to the mysterious thing called Man: "a thing like a tree, whose roots are fed from the earth, while its highest branches seem to rise almost to the stars." (L 132) As the fantastic spires and flying buttresses of a Gothic cathedral express the heights of swaggering pride to which the human spirit can soar, so the bare austerity of a monk's cell reveals the grovelling depths of humility to which equally it can sink. In Christianity there is present the extremes of both pride and humility.

It separated the two ideas and then exaggerated them both. In one way Man was to be haughtier than he had ever been before; in another way he was to be humbler than he had ever been before. In so far as I am Man I am the chief of creatures. In so far as I am *a* man I am the chief of sinners. All humility that had meant pessimism, that had meant man taking a vague or mean view of his whole destiny — all that was to go. We were to hear no more the wail of Ecclesiastes that humanity had no pre-eminence over the brute, or the awful cry of Homer than man was only the saddest of all the beasts of the field. Man was a statue of God walking about the garden. Man had pre-eminence over all the brutes; man was only sad because he was not a beast, but a broken god. The Greek had spoken of men creeping on the earth, as if clinging to it. Now Man was to tread on the earth as if to subdue it. Christianity thus held a thought of the dignity of man that could only be expressed in crowns rayed like the sun and fans of peacock plumage. Yet at the same time it could hold a thought about the abject smallness of man that could only be expressed in fasting and fantastic submission, in the grey ashes of St Dominic and the white snows of St Bernard ... in short, Christianity got over the difficult of combining furious opposites, by keeping them both, and keeping them both furious. The church was positive on both points. One can hardly think too little of one's self. One can hardly think too much of one's soul. (I 155-7)

This Christian balancing act, this juggling with opposites without necessarily dropping any of them, Chesterton traced back not only to a doctrine about the world but to a fact within it. That fact was and is the Christian Church; more precisely, the Roman Catholic Church. It is not, I hope, too neat to say that Chesterton's conversion, though outwardly momentous, was inwardly far less so, since it was really only a conversion from catholicism to Catholicism. Long before becoming a Roman Catholic Chesterton had been impressed by the catholicity of Christianity; the fact that it accommodated, in a seemingly endless series of paradoxes, the apparent inconsistencies of the human spirit: the mild and the militant, the proud and the humble, the austere and the ritualistic. One cannot say the same of the many sects, secular as well as religious, which have offered themselves as substitutes for Rome. In so far as there is truth in them it is likely to be an exaggeration of a truth, unbalanced by any other, formerly found inside the Catholic Church.

Thus a Calvinist is a Catholic obsessed with the Catholic idea of the sovereignty of God. But when he makes it mean that God wishes particular people to be damned, we may say with all restraint that he has become a rather morbid Catholic. In point of fact he is a diseased Catholic; and the disease left to itself would be death or madness. But, as a matter of fact, the disease did not last long, and is itself now practically dead. But every step he takes back towards humanity is a step back towards Catholicism .... The covering or continental character of the Church applies just as much to modern manias as to the old religious manias .... In all of them you find that some Catholic dogma is, first, taken for granted; then exaggerated into an error; and then generally reacted against and rejected as an error, bringing the individual in question a few steps back again on the homeward road. (M 68-70)

Because Roman Catholicism is an old religion, with all the richness and spiritual reserves of an old religion, it has a value not given to any new religion or newly wrought creed. It "saves a man from the degrading slavery of being a child of his age", whereas the New Religions, like new fashions, are all too well suited to their age; and that is their greatest defect.

We do not really want a religion that is right where we are right. What we want is a religion that is right where we are wrong. In these current fashions it is not really a question of the religion allowing us liberty; but (at the best) of the liberty allowing us a religion. These people merely take the modern mood, with much in it that is amiable and much that is anarchical and much that is merely dull and obvious, and then require any creed to be cut down to fit that mood. But the mood would exist even without the creed. They say they want a religion to be social, when they would be social without any religion. They say they want a religion to be practical, when they would be practical without any religion. They say they want a religion acceptable to science, when they would accept the science even if they did not accept the religion. They say they want a religion like this because they are like this already. They say they want it, when they mean that they could do without it.

It is a very different matter when a religion, in the real sense of a binding thing, binds men to their morality when it is not identical with their mood. It is very different when some of the saints preached social reconciliation to fierce and raging factions who could hardly bear the sight of each others' faces. It was a very different thing when charity was preached to pagans who really did not believe in it; just as it is a very different thing now, when chastity is preached to new pagans who do not believe in it. It is in those cases that we get the real grapple of religion; and it is in those cases that we get the peculiar and solitary triumph of the Catholic faith. (M 80-1)

4. Christendom

As Chesterton understood it, a creationist metaphysics is much more than an interesting object of study: it can make a profound difference to the way one views the world; how exactly we attempted to show in the previous chapter. Now we much go further, as Chesterton went further, and as a consequence risk losing many readers. For Chesterton was not content, as twentieth-century convention demands he should have been, to keep his religion to himself. Had this religion of his amounted to no more than a personal vision — the truth as Chesterton saw it — a handful of books and essays would surely have been sufficient to convey its meaning. As it was, of course, Chesterton's religion interpenetrated just about everything he wrote; and the fact that it did so is indicative of Chesterton's conviction that a healthy religion interpenetrates everything we do. This is the conviction that, perhaps more than any other, cuts Chesterton off from the currents of modern life. Most of us are sophisticated enough — one might say, sophists enough — to maintain a cool indifference towards moral views with which our own have little or nothing in common; we are indifferent to them as we are to another's personal taste in food or dress. But what is utterly unaccountable to us is the person who doesn't just profess a different moral viewpoint but practices it, as we say with disdain, 'religiously'; and who does so, moreover, not so much because it is subjectively satisfying as objectively true; true, that is, not just for the person concerned, but for all people.

Why, we ask, with a bafflement born out of this liberal attitude, did Chesterton devote so much of his energy and output to expounding the Christian metaphysic? Why, in book after book, essay after essay, poem after poem — and even in his purely fictional work — did he feel compelled to state and re-state the world view of Catholic

Christianity? It was, when one thinks about it, not merely a distinctly unmodern thing to do. It was also a distinctly unEnglish thing to do. Surely he could have lived and let live, like any decent, well-mannered Englishman? Lawrence Sterne's Uncle Toby in *Tristram Shandy* sums up the Englishman's no-nonsense attitude to religion in his ringing statement that "My Church is the best Church because it never interferes with a man's politics or his religion." And isn't religion for moderns — and modern Englishmen in particular — what the philosopher A N Whitehead said it was, namely something we do with our solitude? It is commonly thought that what prevents more people appreciating Chesterton is his Catholicism. It would be truer to say that what really prevents more people appreciating him — at any rate, in the Anglo-Saxon world — is their Protestantism. There may be nothing left of the latter for most of us but the pious prejudice that our 'value judgments', whether we choose to call them religious or spiritual or simply idealistic, are purely personal and interior to us: nobody's business, in other words, but our own. From which it follows that we do not expect them necessarily to impinge on other people, let alone upon the workings of the world and the institutions that govern it. We are even inhibited from passing on our 'values' to our children: they, like us, must be free to choose their own from the infinite variety which the modern world makes available to them. Each of us today is a member of a sect - of one.

Imagine at the birth of the modern world, around three hundred years ago, some far-sighted atheist musing on how best to deChristianize and secularise society; what better strategy could he have devised than one of 'divide and rule'? When every man is his own Pope, it is impossible for religion to act as a final authority in society; impossible, one might add, for any transpersonal system of ethics to be endowed with authority. From the anarchy of interpretations, which was the first fruit of the Reformation, to the relativity of all values, which is the last, one can trace the continuous process by which religion and ethics alike have been privatised, leaving the world to be governed wholly by utilitarian and technological imperatives. The Manichaean tendencies which we earlier noted as a mark of the modern scientific spirit we can now also see as a consequence of the Protestant spirit. A Protestant may interpret his success in the world as a sign of God's favour. But for Protestantism there is no road through the world to God: by individual faith alone can each of us come to know Him. As for our human reason, it is assigned no more than a practical role in life: it cannot know first truths. It is a faculty for discerning means not ends. To the Protestant, then, the work of man can never also be the work of God; it is without any sacred or ultimate significance. If in Protestantism the world was not exactly the creation of the devil, it might as well go to the devil. In the event, it went to the scientific rationalists whose urge to transform the world took over from the urge to transfigure it. The analogical imagination, which had seen in nature the motives of God, was succeeded by the analytical, which saw there only the motions of matter.

The Reformation, however understandable and even admirable in itself, put Christianity back a thousand years; back to the time when it was just one of the many sects contending for men's souls in the period of Rome's decadence. In seeking, quite consciously, to recapture the purity of primitive Christianity, the sixteenth century Reformers were unconsciously paving the way for a new worldliness. The Inner Light of the faithful, God-fearing citizen might for a time penetrate the outer darkness of a faithless, God-forgetting society. But it was to prove a fitful and flickering light without anything from outside to fan it. There is no denying that the Bible religion of the British has been responsible for a certain conscientiousness in our character which, until recently anyway, coloured our public as well as our private conduct. All the same, a religion of private judgment, inwardness and spirit is bound eventually to claim less and less of our lives. And so it has proved. Technological culture has separated itself from religion, as it has from art, because where there was a mystical there is now only a mechanical materialism. The attempt to sacramentalize the real was given up at the Reformation. To Protestants and rationalists alike there was nothing sacred about nature. There could be no question of profaning it, since it was profane already. We have lost sight of that "minimum of good" in nature, including human nature, upon which Chesterton's optimism was founded; upon which also is founded any idea — whether classical or Christian — of a natural law which isn't reducible to the law of the jungle or the most primitive (thought by moderns to be the most natural) elements of our nature.

The good that is within us is not good enough. For confirmation of which we have only to look around us at the world which, between them, Protestantism and rationalism have created. The brutalization of our arts, architecture and manners, the pollution and despoliation of our earth, the degradation of our sports and entertainments, all bear witness to the heavy price we have paid for desacralizing the world. Sadly, however, the Puritan upbringing of modern Western man has been such as to render him incapable of criticising this world other than in terms handed down to him by a rather arid spirituality. It is arid because, like the Protestantism to which it is distantly related, it leaves the places of the world unwatered. When all ideals, truths, God Himself, are to be found within, what is worshipped without are means not ends, processes not perfections, intermediate not ultimate things. Frog-march the great ends of life to the margins of life, as we moderns have done, and you clear the field for a host of secondary cults to command our allegiance. They parade under various names — Wealth, Work, Efficiency, Service, and so on — but they all have this one characteristic in common, that they are "an idolatry of the intermediate, to the oblivion of the ultimate" (N 7). The busy-man, or businessman, of all modern types, is the one most likely to be found practising and preaching this idolatry. It is indeed with a "worldly asceticism", as Max Weber famously termed it, that he throws all his energy into serving his "vocation" and what he is pleased to call Progress. But Chesterton saw it as an odd sort of service.

> The sin of Service is the sin of Satan: that of trying to be first where it can only be second. A word like Service has stolen the sacred capital

letter from the thing which it was once supposed to serve. There is a sense in serving God, and an even more disputed sense in serving man; but there is no sense in serving Service. To serve God is at least to serve an ideal being. Even if he were an imaginary being, he would still be an ideal being. That ideal has definite and even dogmatic attributes - truth, justice, pity, purity, and the rest. To serve it, however imperfectly, is to serve a particular concept of perfection. But the man who rushes down the street waving his arms and wanting something or somebody to serve, will probably fall into the first bucket-shop or den of thieves and usurers, and be found industriously serving *them*. There arises the horrible idea that industry, reliability, punctuality, and business activity are good things; that mere readiness to serve the powers of this world is a Christian virtue .... All these silly words like Service and Efficiency and Practicality and the rest fail because they worship the means and not the end. But it all comes back to whether we do propose to worship the end; and preferably the right end. (N 7-8)

Chesterton's reaction to the crass materialism of modernity might be summed up as one of fight, not flight It was no good hugging one's spirituality to one's self for fear it would be sullied by contact with the 'world's body'. That was the mistake of Protestantism and all its high-minded successors, among them, spiritualism, idealism and aestheticism. Christianity proper — Catholic Christianity, in other words — cannot simply be a private matter between an individual and his Maker. And this, not only for the pragmatic reason that it then becomes the natural ally of an oppressive secularism, as Luther became the natural ally of the German princes. But also because it hands over the material part of man to the mere materialist or sensualist, as if in Christianity the salvation of the body had no bearing on the salvation of the soul. Granted that Christianity had begun (as it might end) in the catacombs; granted, also, that there was an early element in it which shunned contact with the idolatrous, nature-worshipping cults of pagan Rome; nevertheless its main drive was outgoing and sacramental. It remade men by remaking civilisation. It made Christians as it made Christendom. And it could not have done the one without the other. All the arts and architecture, the holy days and liturgical feasts, the pageantry and pomp and processions of medieval Christianity testify to the fact that it was (in the best sense) a materialist civilization; perhaps too materialist in the end. But in any case it was so because of its civilizing drive: its desire to sanctify the outer world and not just the inner soul. To a still practising Protestant, religion means reading the Bible in chapel, in the family and in private, but it does not entail maintaining or defending a specifically Protestant civilization.

Hence the defence of Christianity could not be for Chesterton a merely private or pious thing. It was bound up, inextricably, with the defence of Christendom. It was, in other words, the defence of an entire way of life: an incarnational civilization in which God was not 'Totally Other' but vividly present to man; present, above all, in the Sacrifice of the Mass and in all the Holy Sacraments of the Church; present in the sacramental acts — from the anointing of a monarch to the blessing of the harvest — which marked the events and seasons of Catholic Christendom; present, finally, in that intricate web of analogies which led men to see physical and material things as the images of a transcendent reality, nature as perfected by Grace. Chesterton more than once likened this sacramental view of the world to the view we have of a stained glass window when seen from within and with the sunlight shining through it. Inside, we are dazzled by the dense colours. But outside there is only lead, dull and opaque, as are all the objects of our senses when unillumined by the divine light. Chesterton is not saying, as the pagans did, that this light hung upon material things. He is saying, rather, that the light shone through them.

> And I think a broad distinction between the finest pagan and the finest Christian point of view may be found in such an approximate phrase as this, that paganism deals always with a light shining on things, Christianity with a light shining through them. That is why the whole Renaissance colouring is opaque, the whole Pre-Raphaelite colouring transparent. The very sky of Rubens is more solid than the rocks of Giotto: it is like a noble cliff of immemorial blue marble. The artists of the devout age seems to regret that they could not make the light

show through everything, as it shows through the little wood in the wonderful *Nativity* of Botticelli. And that is why, again, Christianity, which has been attacked so strangely as dull and austere, invented the thing which is more intoxicating than all the wines of the world, stained-glass windows. (O 60)

For Chesterton, the religion of Christendom did not denote a subject, or even a Bible, which each of us can study privately. It meant an object which all of us can share publicly. Writing of Chaucer's Canterbury Pilgrims, Chesterton pointed to their unity in diversity. The unity is represented by Canterbury; it is what "turned all this crowd of incongruous people into one company" (P 181). Their comradeship sprang from a religion which they regarded, not as a personal intuition, but a social institution. This was the religion that brought such diverse types together, first at the tavern in Southark, then at the tomb of St Thomas of Canterbury.

All modern critics can take pleasure in the almost modern realism of the portraiture; in the variety of the types and the vigour of the quarrels. But the modern problem is more and more the problem of keeping the company together at all; and the company was kept together because it was going to Canterbury.... As their counterparts stand today, it is easier to imagine the Wife of Bath wanting to go sunbathing at Margate, or the Clerk instantly returning, with refined disgust, to Oxford, than to imagine either of them wanting to toil on together to a particular tomb in Canterbury. For the moment, this division of heart is masked by a certain heartiness, in the modern pursuit of mere games and pleasures; but you cannot make a complete social system out of games and pleasures .... There are many modern forces, commercial or scientific, tending to make men look or talk the same. But the Clerk and the Miller did not look and talk the same. They had nothing in common but their purpose; but they had a purpose. (P 182-3)

This modern division of hearts and minds has hitherto been largely masked by a common interest in the goods of comfort, pleasure and security, in supplying which modern industry has proved itself adept. In the absence of a common religion we at least have a common humanity. We may have no heartfelt aims in common. But we do have hearty appetites in common. We also have, to keep us from being constantly at each other's throats, what Chesterton called "the mildness of modern manners". The humanism which consists of a certain common civility and respect for others redresses the sub-humanism of mere appetite. A commercial civilization cannot, as it were, stand on its own feet. It leans heavily upon values which it is not itself able to generate. Chesterton thought these values were too much taken for granted, almost as though they were an ineradicable part of our make-up. But they are easily left to rust in a society which cannot find in its science or philosophy any warrant for them which is not self-serving. As Chesterton observed, our modern attitudes and organization "are in a sense only too natural" and they do not encourage "the really *human* things: will which is morals, memory which is tradition, culture which is the mental thrift of our fathers" (N 16). As a result, against the urgent promptings of desire and self-interest, these human things appear to have little to recommend them. Then, as Shakespeare put it, "everything includes itself in appetite". It is not a pretty sight, but it is one to which modern Westerners have become all too accustomed. Our cities in particular are filled with people in whom any idea of human dignity or brotherhood seems extinct.

How are people to be re-moraliseed: re-educated in the "human things"? Not, thought Chesterton, by any return to the kind of romantic humanism, suffused with a facile religiosity, which was well summed up in the person and this prophecy of Walt Whitman. "I will make unconquerable cities, with their arms about each other's necks", he once cried, "by the love of comrades, by the lifelong love of comrades." The trouble with such sentiments is not in what they express; it is that they are only sentiments. Not being dogmas they swiftly evaporate in the face of stronger sentiments. Modern idealists, in so far as they celebrate the angel and not the ape in man, cannot tell us how the angel got there. And this puts them at a distinct disadvantage in relation to modern 'realists' who have all the weight of modern science and organization on their side, and who can be depended upon to resist any "rally of the really *human* things."

> They herd us like the beasts along lines of heredity or tribal doom; they attach man to the earth like a plant instead of liberating him, even like a bird, let alone an angel. Indeed, their latest psychology is lower than the level of life. What is sub-conscious is sub-human, and, as it were, subterranean: or something less than earthly. (N 16)

By comparison with the inhuman things — in life, as well as in art and philosophy — the human things have not had a good time of it in the twentieth century. This is because the "mystical idea" of human dignity and equality has in our time become no more than a mood — and a passing mood at that. You cannot bask forever in the warm glow of human brotherhood, if you neglect to fuel the fire which is the only real source of this warmth of feeling. Sooner or later the fire will go out, and then we shall find ourselves, morally speaking, in a new ice age, whose coldness and cruelty will be unendurable to humankind.

> The fact is this: that the modern world, with its modern movements, is living on its Catholic capital. It is using and using up, the truths that remain to it out of the old treasury of Christendom; including, of course, many truths known to pagan antiquity but crystallized in Christendom. But it is *not* really starting new enthusiasms of its own. The novelty is a matter of names and labels, like modern advertisements; in almost every other way the novelty is merely negative. It is not starting fresh things that it can really carry on far into the future. On the contrary, it is picking up old things that it cannot carry on at all. For these are the two marks of modern moral ideals. First, that they are borrowed or snatched out of ancient or medieval hands. Second, that they wither very quickly in modern hands. (N 16-7)

They wither because they are not rooted in the firm soil of any creed. The truth is that enlightened optimists have treated a transcendental idea, that of human divinity and dignity, as though it were a natural fact. They have thus been surprised to find that in the twentieth century increasing numbers of men have grown weary of the idea. There are some among us who have more in common with the unpitying hardness of Nietzsche then the extravagant benevolence of Whitman. But even the least ferocious of us would have difficulty in looking at the city crowds with love; more common would be emotions ranging from distrust to disgust. We are conscious neither of any great impulse to love our fellow men, nor of any particular obligation to try. But the idea, that to each individual human soul there is affixed an infinite value, was not dead in Chesterton.

> It remains real for me, not by any merit of mine, but by the fact that this mystical idea, while it has evaporated as a mood, still exists as a creed. I am perfectly prepared to assert, as firmly as I should have asserted in my boyhood, that the hump-backed and half-witted negro is decorated with a nimbus of gold-coloured light. The truth is that Whitman's wild picture, or what he thought was a wild picture, is in fact a very old and orthodox picture. There are, as a matter of fact, any number of old pictures in which whole crowds are crowned with haloes, to indicate that they have all attained Beatitude. But for Catholics it is a fundamental dogma of the faith that all human beings, without any exception whatever, were specially made, were shaped and pointed like shining arrows, for the end of hitting the mark of Beatitude. It is true that the shafts are feathered with free will, and therefore throw the shadow of all the tragic possibilities of free will; and that the Church (having also been aware for ages of that darker side of truth, which the new sceptics have just discovered) does also draw attention to the darkness of that potential tragedy. But that does not make any difference to the gloriousness of the potential glory. In one aspect it is even a part of it; since the freedom is itself a glory. In that sense they would still wear their haloes even in hell. (N 19-20)

You cannot really maintain what is fully human in man unless you also maintain that there is something partly divine in him. You cannot be a real humanist, in other words, unless you are also a real Christian. Secular humanism, in this reading, is an oxymoron. It succumbs too readily to a scientific view of man; whether evolutionist or psychological or behaviourist it doesn't much matter, since all alike lead, so to speak, to a revising downwards in one's estimate of man. Humanism, then, cannot be a substitute for religion. Least of all can it be a substitute for the old corporate religion of Christendom. Piece all the fragments of humanist thought together and you might just arrive at something vaguely resembling the picture Catholic Christendom had of the world. The colours might be a shade wishy-washy and the outlines a bit blurred, as in an impressionist painting, but the resulting assemblage might reasonably be expected to yield a more rounded picture of humanity than is currently vouchsafed to us by any individual fragment alone. Granted all this, there is still the question of who or what is to piece these fragments together so that they again form a coherent and humanly satisfying whole. Chesterton was in no doubt about the answer:

> Humanism may try to pick up the pieces; but can it stick them together? Where is the *cement* which made religion corporate and popular, which can prevent it falling to pieces in a debris of individualistic tastes and degrees? What is to prevent one Humanist wanting chastity without humility, and another humility without chastity, and another truth or beauty without either? The problem of an enduring ethic and culture consists in finding an arrangement of the pieces by which they remain related, as do the stones arranged in an arch. And I know only one scheme that has thus proved its solidity, bestriding lands and ages with its gigantic arches, and carrying everywhere the high river of baptism upon an aqueduct of Rome. (N 28)

There is, of course, a type of humanist for whom the preceding argument carries little weight. He rejoices in the absence of any common standard or "enduring ethic"; in the fact that we each make up our values as we go along. He may even seem like a friend of religion, for unlike the grim atheist he does not ask us to give up our childish attachments. It gives him pleasure to think that everyone can give vent to their moral feelings, provided no one's feelings get too bruised in the process. But when all values are in this way personalised and made non-cognitive all moral conflicts are ultimately irresolvable except by resort to mere assertion. It is then not the best views that necessarily triumph, but, more likely, those which have the greater numbers or influence or powers of manipulation, rhetorical or otherwise, behind them.

There is another type of humanist who does think that some unity may be brought out of the present chaos of opinions. He is the one who, from the rich treasury of Christendom, has plucked out human brotherhood as the pearl most worth preserving. Recognising, too, that brotherhood demands at the very least a minimum of agreement about certain fundamentals, our fraternal humanist looks earnestly for what, at bottom, men have in common. He appeals, in short, to their 'common humanity': the 'essence', he thinks, of all religions. In fact, this attitude is the natural upshot of what in pagan times was polytheism, and in our own is pluralism. Where there are many gods, there cannot be one God. "God", as Chesterton put it, "is really sacrificed to the gods; in a very literal sense of the flippant phrase, they have been too many for him". (Q 104) Where each person or group is free to practice religion on his or its own terms, there can be no true religion; at any rate, in the sense of something which binds us in terms not of our own making but God's. To put it more prosaically, it is very difficult in a polytheistic or pluralistic society to take the claims of Faith seriously. No doubt the pagans thought they were enriching their religious lives when they progressively added more and more gods to their Pantheon. No doubt our contemporary *religiosi* think the same when they seek every opportunity for multi-cultural dialogues and inter-Faith services. But what appears at first as an affirmation of religious pluralism is in fact its denial in the name of a low-key, spiritless humanism, which would liberate people from the embarrassing particularities of their own religious traditions.

This humanism is definable less by what it is for than by what it is against: the myths and memories and rituals of old Western man. It concept of 'humanity' is arrived at, it seems, by subtracting from the human race everything which in the past has warmed and gentled and sustained it. And divided it, the humanist would add. But division — of human types, languages, nations and regions — is the condition of man. From often isolated and local lives, from the subtle shades of meaning hidden in languages and regional dialects, from the songs and epics and folk memories of wandering tribes who have finally come to settle in places afterwards hallowed by their presence; from all such obscure attachments have sprung testimonies and teachings and truths — Homeric, Hebraic, Christian — which most of us recognize as the highest definitions of our humanity. But the humanist can only offer us the lowest definitions of our humanity. 'Natural Man', he tells us, is a simple, asocial-like creature, unencumbered by 'irrational' loyalties and loves, and moved only by the most elementary drives: for warmth, security, and shelter. Now it is obvious that human beings thus reduced to their basic drives do have many things in common. But if these things really do constitute our 'common humanity' they tell us next to nothing about our humanity, save only that it shares certain natural experiences with the animals. Even the cave-man, as Chesterton reminds us, was not so rude and recently evolved as to be governed solely by the urge for self-preservation. He may have wielded a club; but we know for certain he also wielded a paintbrush. We know from the drawings of animals he sketched and coloured on the walls of his caves that "this creature was truly different from all other creatures; because he was a creator as well as a creature" (Q 34). Already in prehistoric times "something of division and disproportion has appeared; and it is unique. Art is the signature of man" (Q 32). Whatever natural feelings or instincts man may share with the animals, it is only in the former that they generate the creative expressions of art and religion.

Now it is precisely the point about modern humanism, as Chesterton saw it, that it is founded on an indifference to the uniquely human; even one might say a horror of the human. Instead, nature is held up as the mirror in which human beings are invited to see their true selves. This 'nature', since the seventeenth century, has reflected back nothing of man's higher aspirations. Rather, it has been a place of impersonal drives and laws utterly alien to human experiences of love and reverence and ultimate fulfilment (or salvation). And yet it is the 'natural' in this sense which humanists have set up as the final arbiter and judge of our mores and modes of life. Whether we are bidden to embrace a playful polytheism, or pluralism, picking at random the religions or 'life styles' which suit us, or sink all such moral differences, together with the "motley humours of humanity" (R 239), in some cosmopolitan common-wealth, the outcome in either case is not a raising, but a lowering, of the traditional ends of humanity. For it is on the level of our 'natural' appetites that we are being invited to organise our lives and societies, with the choice of spiritual as much as material goods constantly at the mercy of our mercurial tastes and temperaments.

Modern society is thus turned into a paradise for consumers, the sovereignty of whose wants is absolute. The public world of such a society — its polity as much as its economy — is wholly given over to utilitarian and calculable considerations, while the private is where the spiritual still ekes out a precarious existence; precarious because it is seen at best as a purely subjective phenomenon, at worst as an epiphenomenon masking more basic drives of an economic or erotic sort. One is bound to wonder whether this privatisation of the Good is not accompanied by a privation of good, which was the old medieval scholastics' definition of evil. It is in any case evident that modern society can find no place, except on its margins, for those serious souls whose 'narrow-mindedness' impels them towards some idea of moral community. Now it so happens that true believers are invariably disturbers of the peace. And, as secular humanists never tire of telling us, much blood has been spilt - indeed continue to be spilt — in the name of True Religion and Virtue. And it was on the ruins of a Europe exhausted by religious wars that the modern, secular state arose. Thus every attempt to re-assert the claims of religion is met with a standard history lesson, intended to show the perils of such a retrograde step.

Chesterton was not intimidated by these accounts of our supersti-tious past into a mute acceptance of the Whig version of history (as Sir Herbert Butterfield called it). He did not believe that the past was "most truly pictured as a thing in which ... our own religion fades away into the religion of the world" (Q 303), or in which the daylight of the gods fades into twilight, the Saint becomes a sceptic, and the crusader a tourist. This progressive, linear view of history is only plausible because of what it leaves out: the great reversals and turnabouts of history. It is also a peculiar reading of the past which leads us to take such a dim view of it. In his anxiety to justify the present and to praise liberal, commercial society, the Whig historian merely confirms us in our modern prejudices. Perhaps it is true (though it is a highly contestable truth) that the neutralisation or dilution of religion has resulted in a greater degree of social harmony. Perhaps it is only in the infancy or immaturity of their race that men have thought it worthwhile to war with one another over ultimate things. We modern men have 'come of age' and so can only sneer at a God of Israel who was also a God of Battles, or smile superciliously at the quarrelsome Greeks, "that labyrinth of little walled nations resounding with the lament of Troy" (Q 88). Chesterton, by contrast, thought - like the men of the past - that the only wars worth fighting were religious wars. And what, he wondered, would be our inheritance today if our forebears had been as pacific and broadminded as the decent, godless men of the twentieth century are supposed to be? Well it is for the world that certain peoples at certain times did not choose the primrose path of compromise and vacillation. Consider the Jews:

Through all their wanderings, and especially through all their early wanderings, they did indeed carry the fate of the world in that wooden tabernacle, that held perhaps a featureless symbol and certainly an invisible god. We may say that one most essential feature was that it was featureless ... It is a typical example of one of those limitations that did in fact preserve and perpetuate enlargement, like a wall built round a wide open space. The God who could not have a statue remained a spirit ... It would have been easy enough for his worshippers to follow the enlightened course of Syncretism and the pooling of all the pagan traditions. It is obvious indeed that his followers were always sliding down this easy slope; and it required the almost demoniac energy of certain inspired demagogues, who testified to the divine unity in words that are still like winds of inspiration and

ruin. The more we really understand of the ancient conditions that
contributed to the final culture of the Faith, the more we shall have a
real and even a realistic reverence for the greatness of the prophets of
Israel. As it was, while the whole world melted into this mass of
confused mythology, this Deity who is called tribal and narrow,
precisely because he was what is called tribal and narrow, preserved
the primary religion of all mankind. He was tribal enough to be
universal. He was as narrow as the universe.

In a word, there was a popular pagan god called Jupiter-Ammon.
There was never a god called Jehovah-Ammon. There was never a
god called Jehovah-Jupiter. If there had been, there would certainly
have been another called Jehovah-Moloch. Long before the liberal
and enlightened amalgamators had got so far afield as Jupiter, the
image of the Lord of Hosts would have been deformed out of all
suggestion of a monotheistic maker and ruler and would have become
an idol far worse than any savage fetish ... that poets and philosophers
can still indeed in some sense say an Universal Prayer, that we live in
a large and serene world under a sky that stretches paternally over all
the peoples of the earth, that philosophy and philanthropy are truisms
in a religion of reasonable men, all that we do most truly owe, under
heaven, to a secretive and restless nomadic people; who bestowed on
men the supreme and serene blessing of a jealous God. (Q 105-8.)

It was because in the past some men were narrow-minded that we
moderns can afford to be broadminded. Which is why it is itself an
instance of narrow-mindedness (not to say impiety) to imagine that
always and everywhere an easy liberality is the best prescription,
whereas in reality it is a luxury which only those secure in their
convictions can afford, and then only in the knowledge that others
once had to fight for them, and one day may have to do so again.
Christianity, for example, has bequeathed much to liberalism,
though little thanks it now gets for it. But that it has done so at all
is due, ultimately, to the unyielding stance which the early Christians took towards alien gods and powers.

Christians were invited to set up the image of Jesus side by side with
the image of Jupiter, of Mithras, of Osiris, of Atys, or of Ammon. It
was the refusal of the Christians that was the turning-point of history.
If the Christians had accepted, they and the whole world would have

certainly, in a grotesque but exact metaphor, gone to pot. They would all have been boiled down to one lukewarm liquid in that great pot of cosmopolitan corruption in which all the other myths and mysteries were already melting. It was an awful and an appalling escape. Nobody understands the nature of the Church, or the ringing note of the creed descending from antiquity, who does not realise that the whole world once very nearly died of broadmindedness and the brotherhood of all religions. (Q 202.)

Hence, to the rule which modern history appears to support, that a polytheistic or pluralistic society inevitably presages an agnostic or nihilistic society, the ancient history of Jews and Christians provides some notable exceptions. The polytheism of Palestine and the Roman Empire was eventually succeeded by the mono theism of Judaism and Christianity. As for such exceptions in modern times, they are not of the kind to encourage those who, like Chesterton, support a spiritual authority alongside the secular. Where today, we still find strong spiritual convictions undimmed by the co-habitation in the same area of two or more powerful religions, we also find that the area is destined by its divisions to suffer bloody conflict, partition or a rule which is alien (often literally) to any of the native religions. The last-mentioned 'solution' — which normally entails a thoroughgoing secularisation, whether imposed by modernisers from outside or inside the country — is bound to seem the most rational to Westerners who themselves have long outgrown such atavistic attachments. Jerusalem, which Chesterton visited in the immediate aftermath of the First World War, remains to this day the paradigm case of an area whose inhabitants, while being divided along the lines of religion, also refuse to be reunited along the lines of irreligion. Chesterton, far from shrinking from this phenomenon, in the priggish manner of moderns, sought to explain it in its own terms.

The truth is that the things that meet to-day in Jerusalem are by far the greatest things that the world has yet seen. If they are not important nothing on this earth is important ... They are ... the things about which the only human sort of history is concerned; great memories of great men, great battles for great ideas, the love of brave people for beautiful places, and the faith by which the dead are alive. It is quite true that with this historic sense men inherit heavy responsibilities and revenges, fury and sorrow and shame. It is also true that without it men die, and nobody even digs their graves ... Their entanglements are tragic, but they are not trumpery or accidental. Everything has a meaning; they are loyal to great names as men are loyal to great nations; they have differences about which they feel bound to dispute to the death; but in their death they are not divided.

Jerusalem is a small town of big things; and the average modern city is a big town full of small things. (S 110-13.)

It was by no means obvious to Chesterton, as apparently it is to so many moderns, that men stripped of their ancient cultures, memories and prejudices, and hence (it is presumed) of their rivalries, will be the better or the more morally knowledgeable as a result. An undifferentiated humanity — the kind of humanity proposed by secular idealists as a solution to the world's as well as Jerusalem's conflicts, a humanity reared on the debris of all existing moral systems — such a humanity may have no common values at all to speak of; rather we can easily conceived of it relapsing, animal-like, into a state of contented indifference to anything but its own appetites. It may be possible, in the manner of Kant, to postulate certain universalizable norms for a creedless society. However, it is one thing to assent in the abstract to the imperative, 'Do as you would be done by', quite another to fill it with content. The bulk of what we recognize as distinctively human, and formative of our moral will, derives from particular traditions and forms of life. Take these away, Chesterton understood, and you take away our humanity. For Chesterton, then, there was no blinking the "chaos of contrasts" which he encountered in Jerusalem, and no overcoming them by some easy formula concocted by those who stand outside all traditions.

These intermediaries everywhere bridge the chasm between creeds as they do the chasm between countries. Everywhere they exalt the minority that is indifferent over the majority that it interested. Just as they would make an international congress out of the traitors of all nations, so they would make an ecumenical council out of the heretics of all religions.

Mild constitutionalists in our own country often discuss the possibility of a method of protecting the minority. If they will find any possible method of protecting the majority, they will have found something practically unknown to the modern world. The majority is always at a disadvantage; the majority is difficult to idealise, because it is difficult to imagine. The minority is generally idealised, sometimes by its servants, always by itself. But my sympathies are generally, I confess, with the impotent and even invisible majority. And my sympathies, when I go beyond the things I myself believe, are with all the poor Jews who do believe in Judaism and all the Mahometans who do believe in Mahometanism, not to mention so obscure a crowd as the Christians who do believe in Christianity. I feel I have more morally and even intellectually in common with these people, and even the religions of these people, than with the supercilious negations that make up the most part of what is called enlightenment. It is these masses whom we ought to consider everywhere; but it is especially these masses whom we must consider in Jerusalem. (S 135-6.)

Of course, Chesterton is not here holding up the Jerusalem of his day as an example of an ideal society. But neither is he saying that its condition would be improved by its inhabitants deserting or diluting their respective faiths, even supposing they could ever be persuaded to do so. Chesterton did not think it odd that men had fought in the past, and would fight again in the future, in defence of their religious beliefs.

The combative religious spirit was never more to the fore than during the Crusades when for a brief period Jerusalem became an outpost of Christendom. But if the Crusades were not a mere destructive war of superstition, as moderns ever since Voltaire have thought them, what intelligible meaning can we possibly assign to them? In strictly geopolitical terms, as Chesterton reminded us, they were a counter movement by Christian Europe against an old enemy. That enemy had succeeded in occupying Roman Spain and had almost conquered Paris. Hence one cannot argue that the

Crusades created, or even exacerbated, a religious difference where previously there had been none; the difference stared Europe in the face in the transformations which Moslems had already wrought there. But Chesterton did not think these facts, or indeed the quarrel between two rival claimants to Jerusalem, a sufficient explanation of the war between the Crescent and the Cross. Something far more fundamental was at stake than the territorial integrity or ambitions of either side. Christians resisted their absorption not simply into the Islamic empire, but into the Islamic creed. They were patriots of religion as well as place; the point being that in the Christian Middle Ages the one was very much bound up with the other. Precisely because of its rejection of idols, and of the Incarnation as itself an idolatry, Islam in its sublime simplicity could not tolerate that hallowing of the world which had gone on as Christianity turned into Christendom. Had Islam conquered Europe, as it nearly did, it would have made a desert of all that had grown up there under the Christian influence. From the isolated deity of the Moslems, little could be deduced of relevance to human society and governance. Those who complain that the Christian Trinity of the Divine Nature is too complex a conception forget that from it sprang the humane complexity — the sanity and balance — of our civilization.

> It was an element in this sublime yet sinister simplicity of Islam that it knew no boundaries. Its very home was homeless. For it was born in a sandy waste among nomads, and it went everywhere because it came from nowhere ... In comparison the Christian civilization ... was full of local affections, which found form in that system of *fences* which runs like a pattern through everything medieval, from heraldry to the holding of land. There was a shape and colour in all their customs and statutes which can be seen in all their tabards and escutcheons; something at once strict and gay ... The mystery of locality, with all its hold on the human heart, was as much present in the most ethereal things of Christendom as it was absent from the most practical things of Islam.
>
> ... It was nothing so simple as a quarrel between two men who both wanted Jerusalem. It was the much deadlier quarrel between one man who wanted it and another man who could not see why it was wanted.

The Moslem, of course, had his own holy places; but he has never felt about them as Westerns can feel about a field or a roof-tree; he thought of the holiness as holy, not of the places as places. The austerity which forbade him imagery, the wandering war that forbade him rest, shut him off from all that was breaking out and blossoming in our local patriotisms. (T 63-5.)

When Chesterton wrote these words there was no very great threat to Christendom from Islam. Nevertheless, in contrasting the two religions he was helping to recall Europe to its substance, or soul; at a time, moreover, when (as he said in his Preface to Henri Massis's book, *Defence of the West*) "by a strange paradox and inversion, we have claimed superiority in everything except the things in which we are superior" (U vii). We have our crusading ancestors to thank for the fact that the wholly transcendent God of Islam did not finally triumph over the incarnate God of Christianity; just as we have the Jews and early Christians to thank for the fact that the immanent gods of paganism did not triumph over the transcendent God of Christianity. In Chesterton's time, and perhaps in our own, the immanent deity reappeared as the more serious of the threats to European humanity. This is the immanent deity of Asiatic mysticism. It is found (so one is led to believe) by a process of introspection, which consists in closing one's eyes and turning fixedly inwards, plunging ever deeper into the depths of one's own self, until finally one merges with the universal self which is the absolute void or unfathomable being of things. This oriental idea, that the sole reality is immanent in each of us, first insinuated itself into the West by way of German idealism and romanticism which (in an understandable but exaggerated reaction against scientific materialism) exalted the primacy of the psychic. However, it has long been apparent that the modern Westerner cannot orientalise himself without relapsing into some form of self-indulgence. His introspection, in so far as it stems either from a lack of any distinct purpose outside himself, or from a wilful refusal to be formed by any objective idea of the Good, invariably leaves him at the mercy of his vagrant moods and appetites, upon which (with the blessing of

Eastern gurus and Western professors) he is all too ready to bestow divine or at least privileged status.

An intellectual abyss separates this view, that the self is everything and everything is the self, from the Christian that our souls are separate from one another, from nature and from God. When the human subject is not identified with the object of greatest desire but can only find it, so to speak, by going outside itself, then and only then do we get the Christian idea of personality as that which can partake (as mere individuality cannot) in the plenitude of being. From the moment of his baptism, when he receives his Christian name, the Western man is bidden, as it were, to make something of himself, to live life more fully, in order to 'rise' to the summits of achievement of which his personality is capable. This is why in the Christian West there has been about every human life the character of a story, whose beginning is given but whose end is obscure and dependent upon how well each of us acts out the drama of his personal existence. Personality, which for the Buddhist is the fall of man, for the Christian is his salvation; it is formed by that process we call soul-making.

The action and the effort of Western man has been directed as much towards his societies as himself. Believing in a God which is distinct from the world he has striven to remake the world in this God's image. By contrast with this dynamic attitude towards reality, we have the inert contemplation and fatalism of the Asiatic sage, who remains (pending his utter extinction) under the sway of the eternal recurrence of things, persuaded in any case by his pantheism that one thing is as good as another. Man's moral and social being has here no leaven with which to renew itself or the world.

> The Indian saint may reasonably shut his eyes because he is looking at that which is I and Thou and We and They and It. It is a rational occupation: but it is not true in theory and not true in fact that it helps the Indian to keep an eye on Lord Curzon. That external vigilance which has always been the mark of Christianity (the command that we should *watch* and pray has expressed itself both in typical western

orthodoxy and in typical western politics: but both depend on the idea of a divinity transcendent, different from ourselves, a deity that disappears. Certainly the most sagacious creeds may suggest that we should pursue God into deeper and deeper rings of the labyrinth of our own ego. But only we of Christendom have said that we should hunt God like an eagle upon the mountains: and we have killed all monsters in the chase. (I 229-30.)

Chesterton's works may be seen as in part a grand attempt to define, and defend, the West anew. Overlaid as it increasingly has been in recent centuries by alien accretions the underlying substance of Western civilization, Chesterton thought, remains Christian and Catholic. And that it does so is due to the very dogmatism which Chesterton cheerfully endorsed as one of the Roman Church's greatest strengths, and which, of course, its critics have always denounced as one of its greatest weaknesses. Time and again in its history Europe has had fits of broadmindedness during any of which it might easily have fallen into one "of those open traps of error and exaggeration which fashion after fashion and sect after sect set along the historic path of Christendom ... But to have avoided them all has been one whirling adventure; and in my vision the heavenly chariot flies thundering through the ages, the dull heresies sprawling and prostrate, the wild truth reeling but erect" (I 168-9).

Humanists and progressives might agree with Chesterton that indeed the Church had been assiduous in hunting down heresies, and that is exactly what is wrong with it. But it was Chesterton's point that that is exactly what is right with it; a point which it is hard not to concede if, with the benefit of hindsight, one is forced to admit that the Church was invariably saner than the ideas she opposed. There must be something, then, to be said for an institution that is, as it were, like nothing on earth.

Now of nearly all the dead heresies it may be said that they are not only dead, but damned; that is, they are condemned or would be condemned by common sense, even outside the Church, when once the mood and mania of them is passed. Nobody now wants to revive the Divine Right of Kings which the first Anglicans advanced against the Pope.

Nobody now wants to revive the Calvinism which the first Puritans advanced against the King. Nobody now is sorry that the Iconoclasts were prevented from smashing all the statues of Italy. Nobody now is sorry that the Jansenists failed to destroy all the dramas of France. Nobody who knows anything about the Albigensians regrets that they did not convert the world to pessimism and perversion. Nobody who really understands the logic of the Lollards (a much more sympathetic set of people) really wishes that they had succeeded in taking away all political rights and privileges from everybody who was not in a state of grace ... In nine cases out of ten the Church simply stood for sanity and social balance against heretics who were sometimes very like lunatics ... A study of the true historical cases commonly shows us the spirit of the age going wrong, and the Catholics at least relatively going right. It is a mind surviving a hundred moods. (N 70-1.)

Chesterton's and Catholicism's critics, even while grudgingly acknowledging the point that in the past the Church might have been right in some of its judgments, can still fall back on the position that people should nevertheless be left free to discover the truth for themselves. This is the familiar liberal argument against any sort of moral authority, the Church's included: no one should accept as true what he cannot demonstrate as true from his own experience. In practice, of course, experience soon tells us that our lives are short and we would make little headway in them if for much of the time we didn't trust to authority, or that accumulated experience we call prejudice. Moderns know this as well as their forebears but are mysteriously reluctant to admit it where moral matters are concerned. Each new generation is supposed to start life afresh, as though its members had been washed ashore on some moral Newfoundland, and had only the processes of trial and error to guide them. Received or 'secondhand' moral knowledge is inferior knowledge which consequently we should avoid handling ourselves, or handing on to our children. And if our own or our children's lives are then ruined or made miserable through moral ignorance, that is the regrettable price we must pay for not impairing our or their freedom. But this argument absurdly presupposes that the millennia of human existence have yielded no certain or cumulative knowledge about how we should live; that, in other words, as T.S. Eliot once put it, we are to "consider the individual ... as a seed out of a packet with no name on it, which we plant and tend out of curiosity to see what it will become." But men in society with a known past are seeds "of a known plant which has been cultivated for many generations - a plant about which we know what its flower or fruit ought to be, if it receives the right nurture and grows to perfection."

Chesterton likewise believed not only that certain eternal truths about human nature had been discovered; not only that they should be taught to each successive generation; but also that the Catholic Church is supremely well qualified to teach them, not least because she belongs to all ages and to none.

> The Catholic Church has for one of her chief duties that of preventing people from making those old mistakes; from making them over and over again for ever, as people always do it they are left to themselves ... it does definitely take the responsibility of marking certain roads as leading nowhere or leading to destruction, to a blank wall or a sheer precipice. By this means, it does prevent men from wasting their time or losing their lives upon paths that have been found futile or disastrous again and again in the past, but which might otherwise entrap travellers again and again in the future ... She does dogmatically defend humanity from its worst foes, those hoary and horrible and devouring monsters of the old mistakes.
>
> There is no other corporate mind in the world that is thus on the watch to prevent minds from going wrong ... There is no end to the dissolution of ideas, the destruction of all tests of truth, that has become possible since men abandoned the attempt to keep a central and civilized Truth, to contain all truths and trace out and refute all errors. Since then, each group has taken one truth at a time and spent the time in turning it into a falsehood. We have had nothing but movements; or in other words, monomanias. But the Church is not a movement but a meeting-place; the trysting-place of all the truths in the world. (M 106-12.)

5. Christian Liberty

All his life Chesterton thought of himself as a liberal; or more simply, a devotee of liberty. And yet he was almost unique among liberals of his time in combining an attachment to liberty with an unfashionable traditionalism of the kind more usually associated with the conservative mind. If this strike the average modern as puzzling or paradoxical it is largely because of the loose way in which liberty has come to be defined, or rather not defined. It is the essence of liberty, we now think, that its meaning cannot be tied down, since it is the very absence of qualifications (or restrictions) which defines it. Liberty, in other words, must mean whatever we choose it to mean; and any other meaning we try and give it runs into self-contradiction.

This modern idea of liberty as content-less, or meaningless, corresponds to the idea of history as progress; according to which men have gained in freedom to the extent that over time they have cast off the arbitrary restraints imposed upon them by priests and kings. The school book or Whig version of history, in which successive generations of Englishmen have been brought up, thus equates liberty with the principle of non-interference. We see this principle first asserted in medieval times by the Barons in their quarrels with the monarchy; then at the Reformation by aristocracy and monarchy alike against the claims of the Church; then in the seventeenth century by the Commons against the monarchy which had created it; and finally in the eighteenth and nineteenth centuries by the landed and commercial classes as justifying their monopoly of power and the uses to which they put it. The triumph of history's progressive forces was widely assumed to be providential, in the quite precise sense of being in accordance with God's purposes for the world; which was all the more remarkable when one considers that the Whig god was also thought to believe in non-interference.

To Chesterton, as to William Cobbett before him, the Whig interpretation of history is a self-serving fable. Granted that a few had seen their freedoms enlarged by the events in the past which progressives glorified, many more had seen them diminished. The removal of Richard II, "following on his failure to use medieval despotism in the interests of medieval democracy" (T 239); the plutocratic pillage by the new Protestant nobility of "things of popular sentiment like the monasteries" as well as "all the things of popular utility like the guilds and parishes, the local governments of towns and trades" (T 173); the defeat of the Stuarts at the hands of the "great Whig nobles who formed the committee of the new regime of the gentry" (T 191); all these events Chesterton saw in a quite different light from that cast on them by the Whig historians. He saw them as stages on the route by which Englishmen have lost the substance of their liberties and retained only the shadow.

English history, in Chesterton's interpretation of it, yields a moral the very opposite of the one which progressives have sought to draw from it. Liberty left undefined, Chesterton said, is liberty left undefended. It is only when liberty is by definition democratic — when, that is, its basis is recognised as lying in a mystical dogma about man's dignity — that there is any security for it. Progress, security, utility: it is to such mundane goods that throughout history liberty has been all too readily sacrificed; and it is in the name of just such goods that all sorts of men — improving landlords, business-men, socialists and social engineers — have claimed liberties for themselves while (liberally) encroaching on the liberties of others. The only solid ground for liberty — the only ground on which it can flourish — is consecrated ground. The concrete liberties of Euro-pean man grew out of the Christian dogma that every man's soul is his own, and that consequently the individual personality has a sanctity, dignity and responsibility beyond anything the economic or political order can assign it. Quite simply, it was Chesterton's belief that this great ideal, which accounted for so much of what was fruitful and socially constructive in medieval times, had not been fulfilled in modern times. The old European idea of liberty as entailing the exercise of real powers and responsibilities, and a space or place in which to exercise them, has not survived the great centralising tendencies of the modern world. Must we therefore accept, since history is progress, that there is nothing to be learnt, let alone gained, by studying what our ancestors made of liberty? Chesterton, on the contrary, insisted that the only way forward was backward:

> The really courageous man is he who defies tyrannies young as the morning and superstitions fresh as the first flowers. The only true free-thinker is he whose intellect is as much free from the future as from the past. He cares as little for what will be as for what has been; he cares only for what ought to be ... If I am to discuss what is wrong, one of the first things that is wrong is this: the deep and silent modern assumption that past things have become impossible. There is one metaphor of which the moderns are very fond; they are always saying, "You can't put the clock back". The simple and obvious answer is "You can." A clock, being a piece of human construction, can be restored by the human finger to any figure or hour. In the same way society, being a piece of human construction, can be reconstructed upon any plan that has ever existed. (V 32-3.)

What, exactly, were the particular features of the medieval social order which Chesterton thought could be applied to modern man's situation? We moderns have been debarred even from asking such a question by our prejudice that anything in the past which cannot be shown as having led to our present isn't worth studying: any such thing is a dead thing, of merely antiquarian interest. Perhaps this prejudice could be justified if our history were a story that had ended well. And there are those among us today, as there were among the Victorians, who think history has "come to an end; if not to a cessation, at least to a consummation." This self-satisfied view, what Spengler called "progress philistinism", stifles criticism every bit as effectively as the most totalitarian regime, especially if it results in the critic of his own times being branded as some kind of a traitor. Chesterton demanded "complete freedom for restoration as well as revolution" (V 32). Chesterton supplied the vital need of his time (and ours) for a politics of the past. It is a vital need because it serves to redress the unexamined assumption of modernists that modern ideas are good because they are modern ideas; which, in turn, presupposes that "we have got all the good than can be got out of the ideas of the past. But we have not got all the good out of them, perhaps at this moment not any of the good out of them" (V 32).

Speaking of medieval ideas, Chesterton said "we must try to imagine, not so much merely what is to be said for them, as to what is to be said against the absence of them" (P 40). We cannot imagine in the absence of organized Christianity — and of its mystical view of man's dignity — how otherwise during the Middle Ages there could have been wrought that immense transformation which slowly turned the slave into a serf and the slave estates of the Roman Empire into the late medieval state of peasant proprietors. Chesterton does not deny that there was long an intermediate state of serfdom, but he also insists that it was not synonymous with slavery:

> This meant that while the land was entitled to the services of the man, he was equally entitled to the support of the land. He could not be evicted; he could not even, in the modern fashion, have his rent raised. At the beginning it was merely that the slave was owned, but at least he could not be disowned. At the end he had really become a small landlord, merely because it was not the lord that owned him, but the land. It is hardly unsafe to suggest that in this (by one of the paradoxes of this extraordinary period) the very fixity of serfdom was a service to freedom. The new peasant inherited something of the stability of the slave. He did not come to life in a competitive scramble where everybody was trying to snatch his freedom from him. He found himself among neighbours who already regarded his presence as normal and his frontiers as natural frontiers, and among whom all-powerful customs crushed all experiments in competition. By a trick or overturn no romancer has dared to put in a tale, this prisoner had become the governor of his own prison. For a little time it was almost true that an Englishman's house was his castle, because it had been built strong enough to be his dungeon. (T 92-3.)

Side by side with the private patches of land the serfs cultivated severally there was the land they enjoyed in common, and normally in common with the Lord. Chesterton described the medieval institution of the Common Land as "an alternative and a refuge ... (the peasants') great green hospital, their free and airy workhouse" (T 93-4).

The parcelling out of productive property, together with the institution of the Common Land, did not come about by accident or mere evolution; it was the fruit of a real moral effort which extended beyond the countryside to the towns where the Guilds stood for the same medieval idea of maintaining a certain rough equality. With this object, they prevented the growth of private monopolies, not by any socialistic scheme of public monopolies, but by setting limits to competition. These limits were severe, as they had to be to ensure not only that a trade should survive, but also that every member of the trade should survive. All alike were subject to the same regulations fixing hours and conditions of work, determining prices and wages, forbidding publicity and enforcing high standards of workmanship. No one was allowed to gain a competitive advantage by producing shoddy goods or adopting cheaper methods of production. Clearly, under this system of communal control private property took priority over private enterprise, from which we can deduce that the quality of things concerned men more than their quantity. Every artisan passed through the grades of apprentice and journeyman on the way to becoming a Master of his particular Art. And it was to the production of Masterpieces, rather than profits, that the whole medieval urban economy directed people. The high standards of craftsmanship, upon which the old Guilds insisted, still "astonishes the world in the corners of perishing buildings or the colours of broken glass. There is no artist or art critic who will not concede, however distant his own style from the Gothic school, that there was in this time a nameless but universal artistic touch in the moulding of the very tools of life" (T 99).

To the idea which Chesterton saw at work in medieval institutions — in "confederations of men with property, seeking to ensure each man in the possession of that property" (T 100) — there corresponded a certain quality which he had loved since childhood: the quality of self-limitation. There glowed in Chesterton's memory the image of the toy theatre which his father had constructed for him as a child, and which all his life served him as "a sort of symbol of all that I happen to like in imagery and ideas. All my life I have loved edges; and the boundary-line that brings one thing sharply against another. All my life I have loved frames and limits; and I will maintain that the largest wilderness looks larger seen through a window" (A 32). Everywhere in the Middle Ages a person's property was hedged round and marked out for him by law and custom. Everywhere in the Middle Ages a person's freedom was restricted: so might a modern critic denounce as a sham or a sophistry Chesterton's claim to have discovered liberty in pre-modern times. But to Chesterton's mind the restrictions were there precisely for the sake of promoting and protecting liberty. Far from testifying to the denial of liberty, these restrictions bear witness to its affirmation by the medieval mind. Its ultimate affirmation was in the sense of the Prayer Book phrase, "In Whose Service is Perfect Freedom." A medieval man could not be a mere instrument of another's will, as he had been on the agrarian slave estates of antiquity. His claim to freedom rested on his first duty to serve God, which, implying good works as well as faith, implied also a social organization which fostered personal responsibility and initiative. To the medieval mind freedom was not the formless, aimless thing it has since become for the modern mind. It was associated with moral order not moral chaos. It meant the erection not the elimination of limits. It was located not anywhere but somewhere. It was something not anything. It was positive not negative. This understanding of liberty, admittedly so unlike our own, found its expression not only in the laws of a Guild, but in the Charter of a Guild:

> By this they had the authority of the King, the central or national government; and this was of great moral weight with medievals, who always conceived of freedom as a positive status, not as a negative escape: they had none of the modern romanticism which makes liberty akin to loneliness. Their view remains in the phrase about

giving a man the freedom of a city: they had no desire to give him the freedom of a wilderness. To say that they had also the authority of the Church is something of an understatement; for religion ran like a rich thread through the rude tapestry of these popular things while they were still merely popular; and many a trade society must have had a patron saint long before it had a royal seal. (T 102-3.)

The point is that the men of the Middle Ages, as Chesterton saw it, attempted "to put some sort of moral power out of the reach of material powers" (N 238). It was a moral power whose presence made itself felt in men's lives: through the Catholic Church and the shrines and saints and holy days associated with her teaching; through the mystery plays performed by the Guilds on the great feast days; through chantry prayers and masses for the deceased. In countless ways the sphere of the secular was surrounded, penetrated and delimited by the sacred. And this made for a freedom to which no completely secular state can begin to approximate.

Most certainly medieval men thought of the king as ruling *sub deo et lege*; rightly translated, "under God and the law," but also involving something atmospheric that might more vaguely be called, "under the morality implied in all our institutions." Kings were excommunicated, were deposed, were assassinated, were dealt with in all sorts of defensible and indefensible ways; but nobody thought the whole commonwealth fell with the king, or that he alone had ultimate authority there. The State did not own men so entirely, even when it could send them to the stake, as it sometimes does now where it can send them to the elementary school. There was an idea of refuge, which was generally an idea of sanctuary. In short, in a hundred strange and subtle ways, as we should think them, there was a sort of escape upwards. There were limits to Caesar; and there was liberty with God. (W 239-40.)

As we know, the "moral power" of the medieval system was eventually submerged under the "material powers" of the modern. And with fateful consequences for freedom. For once freedom loses its foothold in any solid grounding of spiritual principle, it inevitably comes to be identified with the indefinite and unchecked expansion of material appetites: the *libido dominandi* of the monopolist and the power-hungry politician. Thus the economic freedom of modern times, which in theory has been about the right of every man to his own property, in practice has led to the merger of small properties into large and the creation of a propertyless proletariat. The 'free for all' of modern society, in which widely distributed, productive property no longer enjoys the protection of corporate safeguards, has facilitated the rise of a new oligarchy obliged to acknowledge no law higher than itself.

We first see this oligarchy come to prominence at the time of the Reformation, when the spiritual power was absorbed by the secular. It was then made up of improving landlords and merchants who were emancipated as well as enriched by the dissolution of the monasteries and guilds. In matters of social and economic organization, as well as in matters of religion, essentially the same forces were at work weakening the corporate spirit of the Middle Ages and paving the way for that individualist morality which, by removing communal restraints and conceptions, effectively prepared the ground for what Chesterton called a "collectivist plutocracy". The medieval prohibitions on usury and money-making in general could not indefinitely survive the disappearance of the institutions that had upheld them. The fact that they survived at all after the Reformation was due to the association between monarchy and morality persisting rather longer than anyone might have predicted; and certainly rather longer than the merchants of the time thought reasonable. The medieval conception of a just price, and of the subservience of economic activity to ethical standards, was asserted by the Crown and its prerogative courts against the growing opposition of the upper middle class and the Protestant nobility. This, and the Crown's newer claim to regulate Church worship and discipline, were the prime causes of that revolution in the early seventeenth century which led by the end of it to the transfer of sovereignty to an all powerful House of Commons, subject to no laws but those of its own making. England's Glorious Revolution of 1688, which has been well characterised by old Tories as the victory of property over

authority, might with even more accuracy be described by Chester-
tonians as the victory of the modern, Whig idea of fluid property —
that is to say, of the unlimited right to the acquisition and accumu-
lation of wealth — over the older, medieval idea of stable property.
Taking their cue from John Locke, the eighteenth century Whig
Grandees canonised their acquisitiveness, as their nineteenth and
twentieth century successors were to do after them, by identifying
it with the cause of material progress, and of course liberty.

> It is a grim truth that all through the eighteenth century ... Parliament
> was passing bill after bill for the enclosure, by the great landlords, of
> such of the common lands as had survived out of the great communal
> system of the Middle Ages. It is much more than a pun, it is the prime
> political irony of our history, that the Commons were destroying the
> commons. The very word "common" ... lost its great moral meaning,
> and became a mere topographical term for some remaining scrap of
> scrub or heath that was not worth stealing. (T 212-3.)

Chesterton did not think that the modern age was unique in its
abuse of wealth; but in its open and frank worship of the use of
wealth he did think that it differed profoundly from previous ages.
No doubt the medieval corporate spirit was violated often enough;
but at least there was a corporate spirit to violate. By contrast, the
modern spirit of liberty has freed men to buy and sell and trade as
they like, with the result that most men have been dispossessed of
any productive property.

> Capitalism was not only solid, it was in a sense candid. It set up a class
> to be worshipped openly and frankly because of its wealth. That is ...
> the real contrast between this and the older medieval order. Such
> wealth was the abuse of the monks and abbots; it was the use of the
> merchants and the squires. The avaricious abbot violated his ideals.
> The avaricious employer had no ideals to violate. For there never has
> been, properly speaking, such a thing as the ideal good of Capitalism;
> though there are any number of good men who are Capitalists
> following other ideals. The reformation, especially in England, was
> above all the abandonment of the attempt to rule the world by ideals,
> or even by ideas. (N 124.)

Such ideals as still existed in the world Chesterton saw around him were the remnants, often the defensive and isolated remnants, of a social order which had once sufficiently believed in fixed spiritual standards to attempt their institutionalisation. Lacking that institutionalisation, the remnants looked increasingly like oddities, existing more by chance or neglect than design. For example, the professions are just such anachronistic survivals: the character of a profession still has more in common with the medieval than the modern trades; and this by virtue of the rules it imposes on its members, forbidding all manner of unseemly practices. But we forget that, once upon a time, all trades were in this sense professions, and likewise bound by certain rules and standards. It is no coincidence that the professional person is still a substantial figure in his community; someone who stands out as a recognizable type. And this is because the profession, like the guild of old, preserves the dignity and integrity at once of its particular calling and of its members. Chesterton vividly illustrates this point by comparing the respective fates which, in the modern world, have overtaken the Dyer and the Doctor who rode in Chaucer's pilgrimage to Canterbury. Both of them were evidently recognizable (and substantial) social figures in the fourteenth century; but in the twentieth only the Doctor remains so. The Dyer has, as it were, disappeared into the dye-works, becoming an impersonal element in the amorphous productive process; becoming, in fact, the slave, rather than the master, of his instrumental activities.

> The reason why the Doctor is recognizable, and the Dyer is unrecognizable, is perfectly simple. It is that the Doctors not only were, but still are, organized on the *idea* of a Medieval Guild
>
> In the modern doctor we can see and study the medieval idea. We shall not, even if we are medievalists, think it an infallible or impeccable idea. The Guild is capable of pedantry; it is sometimes capable of tyranny. The British Medical Council, which is the council of a Guild, sometimes condemns men harshly for very pardonable breaches of professional law; it sometimes excludes outsiders from

membership who might well have been members. But it does do what a Guild was supposed to do. It keeps the doctors going; it keeps the doctors alive; and it does prevent one popular quack from eating all his brethren out of house and home. It sets limits to competition; it prevents the growth of monopoly. It does not allow a fashionable physician in Harley Street to destroy the livelihood of four general practitioners in Hoxton. It does not permit one professional man to buy up all the practices, as one grocer can buy up all the grocers' shops. (P 73)

It wasn't solely in the professions that the Guild principle of self-limitation could still be seen operating in the modern industrial world. Among small businesses, of the type run by Chesterton's father, there still existed the desire to mind one's own business, rather than someone else's.

My people belonged to that rather old-fashioned English middle-class; in which a business man was still permitted to mind his own business. They had been granted no glimpse of our later and loftier vision, of that more advanced and adventurous conception of commerce, in which a business man is supposed to rival, ruin, destroy, absorb and swallow up everybody else's business. My father was a Liberal of the school that existed before the rise of Socialism; he took it for granted that all sane people believed in private property; but he did not trouble to translate it into private enterprise. (A 10.)

Providence or the very nature of things did not appear to be on the side of such modest ambitions as Chesterton's father nurtured. The creed of expansive capitalism received added impetus in the late nineteenth century from Herbert Spencer's popularisation of Darwin's theory of evolution. By this philosophy, which went by the name of the 'survival of the fittest', a sanctimonious halo was placed upon the heads of Carlyle's Captains of Industry and Finance.

There was a vague idea that the strongest creature violently crushed the others. And the notion that this was the one method of improvement came everywhere as good news to bad men; to bad rulers, to bad employers, to swindlers and sweaters and the rest. The brisk owner of a bucket-shop compared himself modestly to a mammoth, trampling down other mammoths in the primeval jungle. The business man destroyed other business men, under the extraordinary delusion that the eohippic horse had devoured other eohippic horses. The rich man suddenly discovered that it was not only convenient but cosmic to starve or pillage the poor, because pterodactyls may have used their little hands to tear each other's eyes. Science, that nameless being, declared that the weakest must go to the wall; especially in Wall Street. There was a rapid decline and degradation in the sense of responsibility in the rich, from the merely rationalistic eighteenth century to the purely scientific nineteenth. (W 73-4.)

The predatory spirit unloosed by social darwinism might conceivably have burnt itself out but for the opportunities presented to it by developments occurring within capitalism itself. The great shift taking place in the concept of property, from the personal and responsible ownership of tangible things — land, shops, factories, machinery — to the impersonal and irresponsible ownership of stocks and shares, this shift was bound to accelerate the decline of the small business and the small family firm. With the advent of the limited liability company, great corporations could be created, and great fortunes amassed, by speculation. By the end of the nineteenth century, the company promoter had become the cynosure of society, and property his plaything.

Now it is obvious that this condition of society, in which the masses of men are made dependent upon others for their material necessities, and dependent, moreover, on financial speculators with no interest in their welfare, is inherently unstable; if only because the masses of men exist in a permanent state of insecurity, if not always of poverty. By the turn of this century, conservatives and radicals alike were united in the belief that collectivist remedies of the kind pioneered in Bismarck's Prussia were necessary to save the system. Conservative politicians had a hard-headed concern about the effects of under-consumption upon economic growth and England's ability to maintain her industrial lead over other nations, Germany in particular. Hence the reforming Liberal legislation of the late

Victorian and Edwardian periods, notably the Employers' Liability and National Insurance Acts, the establishment of labour exchanges and the introduction of old age pensions, had behind it a broad consensus drawn from all shades of political opinion. As Sir William Harcourt famously put it at the time, "We are all Socialists now."

In such statements, and in the fashionable adoption by all parties of schemes of centralised philanthropy, one catches a whiff of darwinism: the idea that one must adapt, like animals, to changing circumstances. There was little thought given to the possibility that the circumstances themselves might be awry. When "things are in the saddle" we cannot unhorse them; we can only go along with them. So apparently inured were social reformers at the beginning of this century to the conditions of dependence in which masses of people found themselves, it never occurred to them that the conditions themselves might be altered, but only some of the worst consequences arising out of them. It was considered impractical by all parties, when the matter was considered at all, to return to the sort of society in which men are either independent producers or at least exercise some control over their productive lives. The scale of modern production and organization, it was automatically assumed, rendered any such thoughts utopian. And in any case, "you can't put the clock back."

It was fundamental to Chesterton's philosophy that each individual has an immortal soul and destiny, and so cannot be made the pliable material of another's scheme of social salvation. The tyranny of high-minded bureaucrats, Chesterton believed, was set to grow as the frontiers of organised welfare were pushed ever forward to accommodate, not only humdrum matters of pensions and pay, but also the whole question of a healthy nation. The progressive establishment, egged on by the likes of H.G. Wells and the Webbs, increasingly came to think of itself as empowered, by its superior knowledge and insights, to interfere in other people's domestic lives and arrangements. Nowhere was this more evident than in the eugenics movement and in the Mental Deficiency Act, authorizing the incarceration for life of any person deemed mad by two doctors. A Government that was at the disposal of such enlightened experts as eugenists and health faddists, had become itself ungovernable. To Chesterton it was plain that it had lost all sense of proportion. It had lost all sight of that ancient principle of 'subsidiarity', by which power is delegated downwards not arrogated upwards. Instead, what Hilaire Belloc called the modern "Servile State" was claiming the right to take full responsibility for society, and this on the basis that human beings cannot take such responsibility themselves, since, poor things, they are the helpless victims of heredity or environment. Science, not content with the laboratory as a field for its experiments, was now taking the whole of society for its domain.

Eugenics was a species, albeit an especially nasty one, of a larger malady which had infected the modern world. It is that malady which makes the measure of things everything but what it should be. It exalts Progress or Utility or Growth or Survival or Health or all manner of abstract goods; but it does not exalt Man or the good of man. Indeed this malady is marked by the fact that it does not know, and even prides itself on not knowing, what is the good of man; from which it follows that it does not know man. Chesterton made so bold as to affirm that we do know man and we do know in what man's good consists: what are the essentials for a full, free and properly human life. Man is a free moral agent and cannot exercise responsible liberty without the possession of property. The ownership of property, though, does not bestow upon a man that unlimited liberty which, as a matter of historical fact, has destroyed property.

> The special joy of man is limited creation, the combination of creation with limits. Man's pleasure, therefore, is to possess conditions, but also to be party possessed by them; to be half controlled by the flute he plays or by the field he digs. The excitement is to get the utmost out of given conditions; the conditions will stretch, but not indefinitely ... This fruitful strife with limitations, when it concerns some airy entertainment of an educated class, goes by the name of Art. But the mass of men have neither time nor aptitude for the invention of invisible or abstract beauty. For the mass of men the idea of artistic

creation can only be expressed by an idea unpopular in present discussions — the idea of property. The average man cannot cut clay into the shape of a man; but he can cut earth into the shape of a garden ... Property is merely the art of the democracy. It means that every man should have something that he can shape in his own image, as he is shaped in the image of Heaven. But because he is not God, but only a graven image of God, his self expression must deal with limits; properly with limits that are strict and even small. (V 46-8.)

Just as property is the bulwark of responsible liberty, so the free family is its indispensable human expression. "The ideal for which it stands in the state is liberty ... It is the only one of these institutions that is at once necessary and voluntary. It is the only check on the state that is bound to renew itself as eternally as the state. Every sane man recognizes that unlimited liberty is anarchy, or rather is nonentity. The civic idea of liberty is to give the citizen a province of liberty; a limitation within which a citizen is a king" (X 67-8). But this "province", no less than the property which is its foundation, has been much undermined this century. The same restless spirit which has subordinated the fixity of property to the fluidity of property, has also preferred the dramas of promiscuity to the dullness of domesticity. This is the spirit, the *soi-disant* free spirit, which is forever chafing at the bonds by which men and women are attached to a particular place and to each other. This is the spirit which turns men loose and renders them (sometimes literally) homeless. The idea of tying oneself to something, or of a fixed condition freely chosen, was central to what Chesterton called the medieval "civilisation of vows". But it is definitely peripheral to our modern civilisation of contract. Modern society, be it capitalist or collectivist, would much rather deal with mobile, isolated individuals, whether it's for the purpose of employing them, exploiting them, entertaining them, organizing them, reforming them, regimenting them or simply ruling them. An atomised populace, without shaping institutions it can call its own, is shaped instead by the dictates of commerce and government. All sorts of powerful interests and ideologies have viewed the family as a barrier to their programmes of (individual) emancipation. They have pointed to the anomaly of the marriage bond in a world which has shaken off all other bonds except those temporarily forged between people to promote their mutual self-interest. But to enter into marriage as though it were a business contract is to deny, by such calculating detachment, any possibility of enduring attachment.

> Heathen and Christian alike have regarded marriage as a tie; a thing not normally to be sundered. Briefly, this human belief in a sexual bond rests on a principle of which the modern mind has made a very inadequate study ... The principle is this: that in everything worth having, even in every pleasure, there is a point of pain or tedium that must be survived, so that the pleasure may revive and endure ... All human vows, laws, and contracts are so many ways of surviving with success this breaking point, this instant of potential surrender.
>
> In everything on this earth that is worth doing, there is a stage when no one would do it, except for necessity or honour. It is then that the Institution upholds a man and helps him on to the firmer ground ahead ... Coercion is a kind of encouragement; and anarchy (or what some call liberty) is essentially oppressive, because it is essentially discouraging ... The whole aim of marriage is to fight through and survive the instant when incompatibility becomes unquestionable. For a man and a woman, as such, are incompatible. (V 52-4.)

Chesterton was scornful of the idea which has been taken up (from a mixture of motives) by governments, industrialists and suffragettes alike that women denied access to men's work, and hence denied release from the routines of domestic life, were somehow wronged and oppressed. To Chesterton, the woman at home enjoyed something more like emancipation than incarceration. Under the conditions of modern industrialism, he pointed out, men must be in some considerable degree specialists; not so women.

> There is only one way to preserve in the world that high levity and that more leisurely outlook which fulfils the old vision of universalism. That is, to permit the existence of a partly protected half of humanity; a half which the harassing industrial demand troubles indeed, but only troubles indirectly. In other words, there must be in every centre of

humanity one human being upon a larger plan; one who does not "give her best", but gives her all ... She should have not one trade but twenty hobbies; she, unlike the man, may develop all her second bests. This is what has been really aimed at from the first in what is called the seclusion, or even the oppression, of women. Women were not kept at home in order to keep them narrow; on the contrary, they were kept at home in order to keep them broad. The world outside the home was one mass of narrowness, a maze of cramped paths, a madhouse of monomaniacs. (V 126-8.)

The family in its traditional form, like property in its traditional form, embodies ends which are antithetical to the Benthamite utilitarian philosophy. This philosophy is subversive of any institution which does not have as its primary aim the satisfaction of the productive-acquisitive instinct. Chesterton did not think it would much matter whether in the end Big Business or Big Government proved the more effective means of ministering to men's appetites. He only knew that in either event men would have exchanged the substance for the shadow of liberty.

Whatever it is called, there will be no doubt about the character of the world which they will have made between them ... It will be a world of organization, or syndication, or standardization. People will be able to get hats, houses, holidays, and patent medicines of a recognized and universal pattern; they will be fed, clothed, educated, and examined by a wide and elaborate system; but if you were to ask them at any given moment whether the agency which housed or hatted them was still merely mercantile or had become municipal, they probably would not know, and they possibly would not care. (Y 216-7.)

It is tempting to recommend Chesterton today on the grounds of his renewed relevance; to argue, for example, that although Distributism (as his movement for the wider distribution of property was dubbed) can now claim precious few adherents, larger movements in the modern world can still draw sustenance from its philosophy, if not exactly from its programme. Indeed, Fritz Schumacher's pioneering work of the ecological movement, *Small is Beautiful*, grew from an essay originally entitled, *Chestertonian Economics*.

Of the two great modern faiths, from which Chesterton was equally distanced by his own faith, one, the socialistic faith in the beneficence of centralised power, has today all but lost its hold over men's minds. The other, the capitalistic faith in the beneficence of free markets, has yet to acknowledge its foundation in a moral order, and its need (if it is not to undermine that foundation, and therefore ultimately itself) to organize economic life on a more human scale than hitherto it has thought possible, or indeed profitable.

So it may be that the whirligig of time is bringing home to us the relevance of Chesterton. But even if it is not, and even if Chesterton's political and social and religious ideas remain as far from realisation as ever, they would still retain their value; because to know the value of certain ideas — the divine origin and destiny of man, freedom within a closed moral order, well distributed property — is to possess a wisdom which, however the world might despise it, is greatly to be preferred to the cynicism and pragmatism of those calling themselves (mistakenly, as it happens) realists.

Only those who think that history has always to be on their side will shun ideas which do not consort with the *Zeitgeist*. Only those who think that history is always progressing will be afraid to be called reactionary. How tired and stale the progenitors of progress like Shaw and Wells and the Webbs now look! How alive and fresh, by comparison, still seems the perennial wisdom of Chesterton! "Nothing fails like success," said Chesterton. His ideas may have to await a better age than ours to gain the widespread acceptance which is their due; but in the meantime, it is enough that they are etched in our minds, as they were so luminously in his words.

Further Reading

Writings by Chesterton

The most comprehensive list of Chesterton's work has been assembled by John Sullivan's bibliography in three parts, which I understand is shortly to be replaced by an entirely new consolidated bibliography by Geir Hasnes. Two Chesterton samplers that would serve as excellent introductions to him are those edited by W.H. Auden, *G.K. Chesterton. A Selection from his Non-Fictional Prose* (London, Faber 1970), and by P.J. Kavanagh, *The Bodley Head Chesterton* (London, Bodley Head, 1984). Central to any proper appreciation of Chesterton's thought are *Orthodoxy* (1908), *The Everlasting Man* (1925) and *St. Thomas Aquinas* (1933), which last Étienne Gilson, the great Thomist scholar, considered "as being without possible comparison the best book ever written on St. Thomas." There is still no better way of understanding the man than his *Autobiography* (1936), which contains a wonderful evocation of childhood, as well as of the intellectual milieu in which Chesterton led so much of his crowded life. Outstanding among Chesterton's works of literary criticism are *The Victorian Age in Literature* (1912) and *Chaucer* (1932). His *Collected Poems* was first published in 1927. Two of Chesterton's early novels, *The Napoleon of Notting Hill* and *The Man Who Was Thursday,* are still in print from Penguin, as are all the *Father Brown* stories. The first collection of the latter to be published, and generally considered to be the best, *The Innocence of Father Brown*, is also available in an annotated edition by Martin Gardner (OUP, 1987). For an understanding of Chesterton's anti-Whig interpretation of history, *A Short History of England* (1917) and *William Cobbett* (1925) are the indispensable works, the last firmly placing Chesterton in a tradition to which

Dean Swift and Dr. Johnson also belong. Chesterton's social and political views are set out eloquently in *What's Wrong with the World* (1910), and programmatically in *The Outline of Sanity* (1926). Of the second-hand booksellers who specialise in Chesterton, the biggest and the best is Aidan Mackey (15 Shaftesbury Avenue, Bedford MK40 3SA, phone 0234 357760) whose home now also doubles as the Chesterton Study Centre; on display there are bound volumes of *GK's Weekly*, and items of memorabilia. Finally, an ambitious enterprise is now under way in America to publish Chesterton's Collected Works in a series comprising some twenty eight volumes, including all of Chesterton's columns from 1905 to 1936 in the *Illustrated London News* and the definitive edition of his *Collected Poems*, edited by Aidan Mackey, who has tracked down many previously uncollected poems, notably a cycle Chesterton wrote for his wife, Frances, after the death of her sister (Ignatius Press, 15 Oakland Avenue, Harrison, NY 10528. UK orders to Aidan Mackey or the Redemptionist Press, Alfonsus House, Chawton, Alton, Hants.).

Writings about Chesterton

The best introduction to Chesterton is probably still the authorised biography of him, *Gilbert Keith Chesterton* by Maisie Ward (Sheed and Ward, 1944). There is also a subsequent volume, *Return to Chesterton* (Sheed and Ward, 1952), by the same author. There have been numerous biographies of Chesterton since Ward's, most recently those by Alzina Stone Dale, Michael Ffinch and Michael Coren. The most enlightening studies of Chesterton's thought are by Hugh Kenner, *Paradox in Chesterton* (Sheed and Ward, 1948), and by Garry Wills, *Chesterton Man and Mask* (Sheed & Ward, 1961). More specifically, Chesterton's social and political views receive close attention in Margaret Canovan's *G.K. Chesterton, Radical Populist* (Harcourt Brace Jovanovich, 1977) and Jay P. Corrin's *G.K. Chesterton & Hilaire Belloc, The Battle Against Modernity* (Ohio, 1981). For an appreciation of Chesterton's literary approach, there is *On the Place of Gilbert Chesterton in English Letters* (Sheed & Ward, 1940) by Hilaire Belloc, and *G.K. Chesterton: Explorations in Allegory* (Methuen, 1979) by Lynette Hunter. For the fullest appreciation of Chesterton's fictional works, there is Father Ian Boyd's *The Novels of G.K. Chesterton* (Paul Elek, 1975). Father Boyd is also the editor of the quarterly journal, *The Chesterton Review*, published in Canada and obtainable on subscription in the UK from Robert Hughes, 11 Lawrence Leys, Bloxham, Banbury, Oxon OX15 4NU.

Index